John Hewitt was born in Belfast in 1907. A pivotal figure in northern life and letters, he was a poet, an art and literary critic, a political activist and cultural thinker. The foremost exponent of ideas of 'regonalism', his poetic and critical work are widely seen as laying the foundations of the much-heralded 'northern renaissance' of the 1960s. He died in 1987. In the year of his death, the John Hewitt International Summer School was established to promote the poetry and ideals of John Hewitt. His *Collected Poems* (edited by Frank Ormsby) were published in 1991.

TWO PLAYS

TWO PLAYS

The McCrackens • The Angry Dove

JOHN HEWITT

edited and introduced by
Damian Smyth

LAGAN PRESS
BELFAST
1999

The publishers would wish to thank the curator and staff of the John Hewitt Archive at the library of Ulster University, Coleraine, for their assitance in the production of this book.

Published by
Lagan Press
7 Lower Crescent
Belfast
BT7 1NR

ISBN: 1 873687 67 2
Author: Hewitt, John
Title: Two Plays
1999

Cover Design: December
Set in New Baskerville
Printed by Noel Murphy Printing, Belfast

CONTENTS

Introduction

John Hewitt (1907-1987) is known primarily as a poet, a pivotal figure in the literary, artistic and cultural history of that part of Ireland which remained under the jurisdiction of Britain after partition in 1920.

His voluminous writings, in criticism, cultural analysis, cultural politics, letters, reviews and of course, most importantly, poems, constitute a formidable document of radical dissent within the vexed parameters of Northern Ireland. A direct line can be drawn, and indeed was drawn by the poet himself, from the class of men and women who formulated and executed the programme of the Society of United Irishmen in the 1790s to the consistently nagging cultural agenda Hewitt pursued throughout his life, but most energetically in his native province between the years 1942 and 1957.

That period begins with Hewitt reading *The Culture of Cities* and *A Faith for Living* by the American regionalist and thinker Lewis Mumford and ends with the poet's leaving Northern Ireland for a period of self-imposed exile following what he believed was a political and sectarian conspiracy to keep him from the directorship of the Belfast Museum and Art Gallery—a belief given substance by the sequence of extraordinary events which led up to the appointment of a less well-qualified Englishman.

The intervening years had seen Hewitt engaging in a campaign of activism on behalf of his 'regionalism', a solution as he saw it to the age-old tribal divisions in Ireland and, ultimately, a means of gently detaching those Ulster people of 'planter stock' from their attachment to Britain. Central to Hewitt's ideas were an attempt to state in non-confrontational ways the 'rights of tenure' drawn from "the soil and sky;/the use, the pace, the patient years of labour" which belonged to the planters and then to claim a common citizenship by assembling "ancestors of the mind" who could establish and endorse the radical and civic republican ideal which was, in his view, the lasting contribution of the Ulster Protestant to the culture of Ireland.

This agenda was pursued in newspaper articles, radio broadcasts and in major poems such as 'Once Alien Here' (1942), 'Conacre' (1943), 'Freehold' (1946) and 'The Colony' (1950), the collection *No Rebel Word* (1948), as well as in a host of poems celebrating and parsing the places of Ulster, particularly in the Glens of Antrim. It was these activities which, in the eyes of some in the exclusively unionist establishment, made him an undesirable.

But it would be a mistake to see in Hewitt a blind convert to the rituals of Irish nationalism: he was emphatically of planter stock and he drew political and cultural sustenance from the traditions of English radicalism (Cobbett, Morris, the Levellers, the Chartists), those

> ... sturdy folk, the nameless and the named,
> the vertical men who never genuflected,
> the asserters, the protesters,
> like that old Leveller who scratched his name
> in the lead lining of the Burford font,
> *Anthony Sedley prisoner*
> *sixteen hundred and fortynine.*
> —from 'Roseblade's Visitants and Mine'

For though he savoured the ironies of the 'round tower' within his ancestral "planter's gothic" church of Kilmore in Armagh, he was pointedly aware of the inheritance of his own stock:

> we would be strangers in the Capitol;
> this is our country also, nowhere else;
> and we shall not be outcast upon the world.
> —from *The Colony*

So Hewitt's legacy is a complex one, but it is not confused. Like his republican ancestors, Hewitt brought a unique ingredient to the Irish shore: multiple, simultaneous identity, the overlapping of frontiers, the elision of margins.

The two plays published in this volume, in print for the first time, exemplify that cross-fertilisation of imagination. The period from the end of the war until his departure for the Herbert Museum and Art Gallery in Coventry coincided with a revival in the professional theatre in Northern Ireland, due largely to the efforts of managers and actors like Harold Goldblatt and R.H. McCandless in the Group Theatre in Belfast and to the work of George Shiels, St. John Ervine, Joseph Tomelty and, later, Sam Thompson, as playwrights. The theatre was the forum for a host of ideas new to Ulster (many European and American plays received their British and Irish premières in Belfast) as well as an immediate means of reflection on the social and political stresses to which the north was heir; and theatre people were in the thick of cultural debate and discussion, drawn from all sections and classes in the community, socialising and working with writers, painters and agitators.

Hewitt's three public ventures in the drama date from this period. The first of his dramas, *The Bloody Brae*, though begun in 1936, was broadcast on BBC radio in 1954 and given a stage production in the Lyric Theatre in Belfast in 1957. A verse play of substantial rhetorical gifts and emotional strength, it deals with the aftermath of a legendary massacre of Catholics at Islandmagee in Antrim in 1642. Its themes of repentance, retribution and forgiveness made its publication in Hewitt's last volume of poems, *Freehold* (1986), peculiarly far-sighted given the war of bloody attrition that had developed in Northern Ireland between opposing ideological forces and make the play an extraordinary counterpoint to the icy realities to be faced in Dorfman's *Death and the Maiden*.

But it is these two hitherto unpublished plays which reinforce Hewitt's claims as a dramatist of note. Though both texts are held in the Hewitt Archive in the University of Ulster at Coleraine, neither is dated, but it is possible to make an informed guess in both cases. In a letter to Patrick Maybin, a poet friend who was then living in England, Hewitt expressed his dissatisfaction with a play which had opened in the Group Theatre in Belfast in the spring of 1948, objecting to its failure to grasp period politics and to realise adequate characterisations of historical figures. Jack Loudan's *Henry Joy McCracken* was written to mark the 150th anniversary of the 1798 Rebellion and the trial and execution in Belfast of McCracken, its northern leader. The work was professionally revived in 1998 by Centre Stage Theatre Company in Belfast and, indeed, the inadequacy of the playwright's political wit was clear—though Hewitt's assessment of the play was perhaps coloured by his own sense of proximity to the characters and incidents it portrays. Nevertheless, the text here reproduced bears all the marks of a pacy retort to that work. This play is entirely new to the Hewitt canon—it was discovered among papers in the library at Coleraine and, to my knowledge, is not referred to in Hewitt's own notebooks and jottings, in letters in the Public Records Office or in the thorough diaries of Roberta Black Hewitt, the poet's wife. These facts, along with that of a manuscript which is not typed but written in pencil in longhand, lead one to the conclusion that this play was hastily conceived and executed, brought through perhaps no more than two drafts to its present condition. It is certainly not a script which, I believe, Hewitt would have released to the public.

However, this need not be viewed entirely as a weakness of the piece: characterisations in the script are suggested *sufficiently*; principles are declared with some humour and without undue bombast or priggishness; events are alluded to without sacrificing human detail to dramatic spectacle; sympathies are secured through 'personality' rather than demanded through political posturing. In other words, the weaknesses of Loudan's play are entirely avoided by Hewitt's and this can be ascribed partly to the superior imaginative gifts the poet brought to the concept, but also, I think, to the nature of the drafting process.

The play, under the title *The McCrackens*, was given a rehearsed reading at the Eleventh John Hewitt International Summer School at Carnlough, Co Antrim, in 1998 to some acclaim. It was apparent from this reading that it was conceived as primarily a radio play and it was in such a form that the drama critic of the *News Letter* recommended it be given an airing by the BBC in Belfast.

Whereas *The McCrackens*, featuring Wolfe Tone, Thomas Russell, Mary Ann McCracken, James Hope and the rest of Hewitt's ancestry of the mind, is central to his own myth-making as a poet and political thinker, the place of *The Angry Dove* may not be as immediately obvious. A life of Columcille (also known as Columba), may not appear to be an obvious theme for the free-thinking, sceptical poet of Methodist stock. Yet the play works as an impressive imaginative effort to conjure a figure whose influence and personality Hewitt preferred to that of Patrick: Columcille was strong, soldierly, artistic, with none of the mildness attributed to the National Saint. He was also, of course, irrevocably an Ulsterman, and this point is driven home by Hewitt repeatedly in the course of his drama as is the saint's origin in Derry of the Oaks:

> Men at my bidding, since Columba's time
> have packed its story with transcendent crime,
> slaughtered the hostage and betrayed their kin
> and lived by hatred like a discipline.

The force of these lines recall Hewitt at his best. The concept of the play can be seen as an attempt by Hewitt to engage with the pre-Roman Catholicism of the native Irish, finding in Columcille a salutary character who travels well, particularly to the England of Iona and bringing there a more Nature-based Celtic Catholicism which eventually is overcome by the Catholicism of Rome: almost Patrick's journey in reverse and a healthier one in Hewitt's mind.

This play was one of those commissioned by the Ulster poet and BBC producer in London, Louis MacNeice, an exact contemporary of Hewitt's. Another verse play, commissioned and written at the same time, was Roy McFadden's on the mythical Ulster hero Cú Chulainn, entitled *The Angry Hound.* It is not a wild estimate, therefore, to date *The Angry Dove* to the same year, 1952.

As with all of Hewitt's work, the poet speaks best in his own voice. These plays are presented here for the first time to augment the poet's published prose and *Collected Poems* (Blackstaff, 1991).

Damian Smyth
1 July 1999

THE MCCRACKENS

CAST

Henry Joy McCracken, *a leader of the rebellion*
Edward Bunting, *antiquarian and musician*
Theobold Wolfe Tone, *a leader of the rebellion*
Mary McCracken, *sister of Henry Joy*
Thomas Russell, *librarian, a leader of the rebellion*
Matilda Tone, *wife of Theobold Wolfe Tone*
Samuel Neilson, *editor of* The Northern Star
Jamie Hope, *weaver, a leader of the rebellion*
Dr. James McDonnell, *doctor and philantropist*
John Templeton, *botanist*
George Dickson, *rebel, retired ex-soldier*
Paul Douglas, *his servant*
James Orr, *poet, a leader of the rebellion*
John Storey, *printer of* The Northern Star
John Dickey, *rebel, Attorney of Randalstown*
Boy
Dr. Alex McDonnell, *brother of Dr. James McDonnell*
Servant
Dr. R.R. Madden, *author of Lives of the United Irishmen*

SCENE 1

The McCrackens' drawing room. June 1795. Bunting seated by the fire writing—door to right opens. HENRY JOY MCCRACKEN *enters singing.*

> 'Tis pleasant to be in Ballinderry
> 'Tis pretty to be in Aghalee
> But prettier far in little Ram's Island
> Under—

HENRY JOY: Oh hullo, Attie. No, don't go. Just back from a grand day. The others will be up in a minute.

BUNTING: Did ye all come back?

HENRY JOY: No, Attie. The Simms dropped off at their own house and Willie has gone out again. The Neilsons went on home but they'll be in later. There's only the Tones and Tom Russell. So you needn't bolt away like a rabbit.

BUNTING: Oh I know, Harry. But I don't think I ought to stay thrusting myself in among your friends. You'll be having serious and elevating conversation.

HENRY JOY: My friends, be damned! They're yours too, Attie. They love the wondering air ye catch and every wheeple tune that's Irish'll have them yer slaves forever.

BUNTING: Yes, that's what I'm really afraid of. They'll ask us to play them something and Mr. Russell will sing.

HENRY JOY: Now Attie, now. Tom's voice is alright.

BUNTING: At the Mudlers maybe but not in a drawing room. Still I'm glad the Simms didn't come back with ye. I see enough of them and their smug daughter breaking my heart on a pianoforte at five shillings a lesson.

HENRY JOY: Ye should have taught the harp, Attie.

[*Enter* WOLFE TONE, RUSSELL, MRS. TONE, MARY ANN MCCRACKEN. BUNTING *rises.* HENRY JOY *and* BUNTING, *backs to fire, greet oncoming group.*]

TONE: Harp did I hear ye say? Or was it you, Harry?

BUNTING: Good day, Mistress Tone. Good day, Mr. Russell. Mary me girl, I've missed you round the house. Was it a good day ye had?

MARY: It was a grand day. [HENRY JOY *singing*]

BUNTING: Aye, I heard him at it when he came in.

[TONE *and* HENRY JOY *converse.* MRS. TONE *and* RUSSELL *who finds her a chair.*]

RUSSELL: Mary, shall I fetch ye a seat beside Mrs. Tone?

MARY: Aye, do Tom, please.

[BUNTING *seated in corner left over fire.* HENRY JOY *and* TONE *stand before fire.* MRS. TONE *and* MARY *with* RUSSELL *standing in attendance. They are suddenly silent.*]

TONE: Mr. Chairman, Ladies and gentlemen. I will now call upon that inimitable orator, Mr. Hutton, to—

HENRY JOY: No politics now—Bunting you know is now a fully-fledged Tory ... and stays here on that understanding, don't you Attie? One bugle call, one party cry and the hare's away over the hill.

MARY: Not hare, Harry—skylark, thrush or something with music in it.

MATILDA: I hate the word too. Hare. I always think of harelip.

TONE: Tush, Harry, I'm surprised by so low an estimate of my versatility—politics isn't my only store—there's astrology, astronomy, botany, geology, mythology. [*To* RUSSELL] Sorry PP, I forgot I wasn't a librarian.

RUSSELL: I never can remember that I am one.

HENRY JOY: I say Hutton, you're a damned lucky fellow. I'm just beginning to realise how lucky you really are. Here we are in Belfast, surrounded by 20,000 of the dullest dogs conceivable— and we, the legion of light, the playboys of the spirt, the witty ones, we must save the Protestant rabble, the dissenting horde— Bunting here teaches their daughters the piantoforte and charms their fat little souls on Sunday with his skill, PP lends novels to their wives for tedious afternoons and winter evenings when there isn't a dance or a ball. And I sell them shirts!

MATILDA: But Harry! Shirts are a useful commodity.

HENRY JOY: Don't interupt, Matilda, please, and here are you, Hutton, with a bag of gold and a pretty wife and not a care in the world.

TONE: Easy, Harry, easy. Three children, a blank future and a wife's sister—not a care in the world!

RUSSELL: Blank future—America—a new civilization.

MATILDA: Now PP don't start your hobbyhorse building—democracy's in the air—the People's Free State of the west—I know you of old—d'ye know Mary this tall soldier, this scholarly librarian, this geologist this Templetonian—is at best a shy little boy dreaming dreams in his classroom of a turretted rainbow.

RUSSELL [*wagging a solemn finger at* MATILDA]: Shy or no, I could cook chops, dreamer or not I can make a pie, in full lace regimental uniform too.

BUNTING: Harry, you miss the real tragedy in this bargain, this buying and selling. You make your cloth and have done. You needn't wear the shirts ye make. I must sit and list to the Misses Simms.

MARY: Harry, my dear, I think the rural air of the Falls Meadows is making you light-headed ... Here we are with the celebrated Mr. Hutton itching to address us and the famous Mr. Bunting dying to play for us and you keep talking of the cotton manufactory you're supposed to manage but seldom see. Ye'd think nobody had ever worked for his living before. [HENRY JOY *protests.*] Matilda, dear, would you like to hear the celebrated Mr. Hutton—

MATILDA: I'm sure Mr. Hutton is really tired speaking. He's done plenty this week. He's had that big gathering of delegates. Oh, I'm sorry—

BUNTING: It's quite alright, Mistress Tone. I knew about that—yer not letting anything slip out at all. Ye couldn't live in this house and not know what was happening—

MARY: Come, Attie, that's not true. Why my mother knows nothing of it. I don't perpetually insist on my responsibilities to the fair sex of this town with regard to the important question of muslin and dress materials.

HENRY JOY: What is really in my mind is the firm necessity for every professional incendiary to have a private income. One can't overthrow the British Empire in one's spare time.

TONE: I know. That's why Neilson is such a perfect Jacobin. Making

his fortune first out of wool and then settling down to run *The
Northern Star.* That's good business. Unfortunately, none of the
learned professions offered me that opportunity and I can't
imagine myself in trade.

MATILDA: Fie, Theo! Your brother hasn't your scruples or
refinement. You might have shared his manufactory scheme
with him.

TONE: Tush, my dearest love. If you're anxious on a turbulent
ocean of commerce, Mary here will make you her American
agent and representative. PP here couldn't abide his magistracy.
I think Tom is very happy delighting the studious Dr. McDonnell
and the diligent Mr. Templeton with his learning and charming
the young females with the elegance of his address.

RUSSELL: Hutton, you are unfair. Grossly unfair. Harry is more
overpowering with the ladies and those of more than in one
station and rank—

HENRY JOY: Tom, if it's that gamekeeper's girls you're thinking of—
it's only my patriotism that intrigues 'em.

MARY: I'm glad that our tragic nation has such devoted daughters.
If either of you two gallants can suggest any more susceptible
females—susceptible to the lofty claims of national dignity—I
shall surely inaugurate a new and allied Society of the United
Irishwomen—with Matilda as President and Commander-in-
Chief.

TONE: If ye'll pardon the impropriety, I'd say she'd make a better
Commander-in-Chief than one I could name.

BUNTING: I've been listening to ye with the utmost care and can't
help finding two queries forever rising to me mind.

HENRY JOY: Out with 'em, Attie, my boy.

BUNTING: First, this talk of professional incenduries and
overthrowing the Crown—I remember, Mr. Tone, when you
came to Belfast first it was far otherwise you talked.

TONE: I've been educated by events, that's all. It was emancipation
I clamoured for then.

BUNTING: And Lord Kenmare in the name of his fellow worshippers
repudiated your solicitude—

HENRY JOY: Don't speak of that! I feel my gorge rise still.

RUSSELL: He should have been called out.

MARY: Tom, Tom.

BUNTING: I tell ye. You all misgauge events and you live and move in a revolutionary atmosphere and your fine flowers of rhetoric—Rights of Man, Independence—wilt and wither on the real cold air of the villages and lanes—they flourish only in the heated air of tearooms and clubs—

MARY: Attie, I haven't heard ye so eloquent before.

TONE: It's alright, Mary. We shall deal with him when he's finished.

BUNTING: I am an ordinary citizen, a law-abiding one withal. I do not hate the Catholics. My love for this country has been proved in many—

HENRY JOY: Concert rooms.

MARY: Harry, be still.

BUNTING: But I can see no alleviation of the plight of those ye call the oppressed classes until they are educated to extract the full benefits of progress.

RUSSELL: How can they ever be educated while they are yet enslaved? I would have them rise before the last elements of humanity have been ruthlessly crushed out of their wretched bodies.

TONE: Aye—every window and every head at the mercy of Orange stick and stone with not a petty jury to convict.

MARY: And not Catholic windows only. Remember McCabe, Attie?

BUNTING: I still cling firmly to my belief. Frankly, Washington and Paine can mean nothing to them. And your fine French theories are beyond their wit and grasp.

TONE: I don't speak to them of theory and absolute. I say 'Are ye not hurled out of your little farms to make room for Protestant freeholders who can assist their landlords by shotgun and vote. Is the little acre safe that your grandfather dug and your father ploughed, when the lease draws to its close?'

BUNTING: But prejudice shouldn't blind you sir to the truth that they are unprofitable and lazy.

HENRY JOY: Ye forget the need for the Hearts of Steel as well as the Peep O' Day Boys.

BUNTING: And then the government falls upon them with its dragoons and yeomanry—why if ye were all law-abiding, they could even dispense with the castle spies.

TONE: Nonsense. It is a conquered land and has to be held by force and subterfuge.

BUNTING: You compel them to use arms and the rigour of the law and state against ye. Did ye but ask for the goodwill of His Majesty?

TONE: Goodwill be damned.

RUSSELL: What of Fitzwilliam's vice-regalry? Didn't he attempt just the things we wanted, the emancipation, the reform of Parliament and the expulsion of Beresford and his gang? And what happened? King's representative or not he had to go—driven out by Pitt and Beresford. No emancipation, no reform. I tell you when Fitzwilliam left Dublin, in the same vessel left Ireland's last chance of constitutional salvation—There's only one way now, by the arming and rising of the Catholics and Dissenters to achieve the independence of Ireland from the English Crown, the republic of democracy and the people's ownership of the land.

MARY: Bravo, Tom! Ye'v listened to Jamie Hope to good purpose. He'd have cheered that last remark to the echo.

HENRY JOY: Ye may mislike Jamie's brusqueness and want of humour but on the people and the land and the war of the classes as he calls it there's none to approach him for clarity or vehemence.

BUNTING: I can't see your Mr. Simms or your Mr. Sinclair march out to battle with weavers and ploughboys for the egalitarian republic, in spite of what you say!

TONE: Nor can I—though they might against Parliamentary abuses and the freedom of trade—but what was the second idea, Attie? Or have we smashed both in our devastating onslaught?

BUNTING: I survive, Mr. Tone, I survive. Let me protest my affection and esteem for ye all. I think ye mistaken but mistaken or no you're better company than a coachload of camdens. So ye'll not misunderstand my next assault. It pains me to hear such gentle and talented people, such witty and cultivated companions, view with equanimity—even not without a certain joy—the plunging of this land into a sea of fratricidal strife. I fear me, it's a peculiar failure of imagination that permits wild talk of incendurism and civil war.

HENRY JOY: But Attie, you goose, the war is on and not of our making. Norbury goes on circuit and of 98 prisoners, 97 are executed—the acquitted one, a soldier who has murdered a peasant—

BUNTING: Aye, I'll admit that these are wrong but is the way to right it to fill the harbours with French men o' war?

TONE: You hit at me. What of Corsica then? It is virtue and honour for them to invite the protection of his Britannic Majesty but for us to attempt the same gesture is bloody treason and cursed malignity.

MARY: Matilda, I'm sure you would like to hear the celebrated Mr. John Hutton discourse with the amiable Mr. Russell on the intricate devices of geology for a change—

MATILDA: What I really wanted to say was that Mr. Bunting's music would be much more acceptable to me.

TONE: Magnanimous, I yield, O Son of the Sassenach.

RUSSELL: Will it be a song you play, Bunting, or—

HENRY JOY: There he goes, Attie.

MARY: Tom has a charming voice, Harry, I'm sure.

RUSSELL: I—I never suggested—

BUNTING: Here I've been a prisoner in town all day: teaching dull little Misses their scales and hoping to sell a piano to a vulgarian who wants music and taste and thinks because he's got money— you've all been romping and gambolling in the sun listening to the lapping water, the wind in the grasses, mabbe a lark or two—and ye want to hear me and my disgruntled spirit crying out. Tell me, Harry, did ye come back by Aghalee that you're singing about and how's the apple-blossom or is it too early yet?

RUSSELL: Patriot to the core. It is the County Armagh that you're thinking of.

HENRY JOY: Versatility or not, Mr. Hutton, we all come back to Ireland by every road we take and you'll come back yourself.

TONE: I don't yield to anyone on the point of patriotism but the Americas shall have the honour of sheltering my bones and my son's son will walk the lanes of Pennsylvania and feel the sod friendly beneath his heel, a free man native in a free land.

MATILDA: I hope so but sometimes I get a little afraid. It's—so far we have to travel, a thousand leagues.

MARY: Harry, you scamp, you do say wise things once in a while. I must remember that—'We all come back to Ireland by every road we take'. Tom, you have come a long way yourself.

HENRY JOY: Oh Mary, Mary, you're romantic. The east got too hot

for him—Attie, come and play us something thoroughly
miserable so we can cry outright. [*Rap at door. Enter* NEILSON.]

NEILSON: Sorry, I was so late.

MARY: Isn't Mrs. Neilson with you?

NEILSON: No, Mary. The journey was a trifle tiring for her and she
felt the wee fellow needed her. She'd neglected him so long.

MARY: Oh, I'm sorry. I was looking forward to continuing our tête-
à-tête so rudely interrupted by our arrival in town.

NEILSON: Hello, Attie. You're the only one I need to greet. I have
had the pleasure of these other men's company practically all
day.

TONE: Isn't even Bunting a gentleman or does the Jacobin insist on
consistency?

NEILSON: He does.

HENRY JOY: You're dashed lucky, Sam. Tom's just tuning up, he's
about to sing.

RUSSELL: Harry boy, you are a devil—I wasn't at all.

MARY: Actually, Attie was on the point of playing us a new piece.

BUNTING: None of my pieces is exactly new, Mistress Mary.

NEILSON: Ye'll surely give us the 'Marseilles' chorus and that's new
enough.

HENRY JOY: Why must we go to the French for a song?

MATILDA: Well heaven knows our ideas are French enough!

RUSSELL: Come, Matilda. Paine is an Englishman and I consider
him of more significance than any of the encyclopedians, good
as they are.

HENRY JOY: Now Tom, don't recite 'These are the times that try...'

RUSSELL: And why not? These *are* the times that try men's souls.

BUNTING: Here's one guaranteed Irish and as good as any war song
of the Rhine.

MATILDA: What's it called?

BUNTING: 'The Little Red Fox'. I got it from the man with two
heads.

HENRY JOY: Poor old Dennis. Voice from the past.

NEILSON: I'm still sorry it's not the 'Marseilles'.

RUSSELL: He'll play it yet. We all know the words.

HENRY JOY: *Allons mes enfants*—forestall ye that time Tom me boy.

MARY: Harry, be quiet, Attie's about to begin.

[BUNTING *plays* 'The Little Red Fox', 'Let Erin Remember' *in quick time.*]

HENRY JOY: God, to be marching at the head of 20,000 men to that tune.

TONE: Brave Attie. It's grand.

MATILDA: So, Harry, you do think the musician has his use!

HENRY JOY: Of course, after the blacksmith has done his share and then again after the battle's over.

TONE: Aye. 'The Flowers O' The Forest', mabbe.

BUNTING: Thank ye. Do ye know I feel it in my bones that I'll do more for Ireland than any one of ye—saving your pardons—for I rescue and preserve little shreds of song, little wistful ditties that will outlast yer drums and cannon, that'll sing themselves into the hearts of men and set Ireland free because her soul is free.

RUSSELL: But bodies must first be free.

BUNTING: A flare in the dark, a pike thrust and a scream, a curse and a volley. Can ye see any more on the road ye want to travel?

HENRY JOY: Nonsense. I see small happy homesteads on the hills. I see the people dancing at the crossroads, Catholic and Protestant hand-in-hand. I see happy childer singing in their bright schoolrooms ... No more Rapparees, no more Peep O' Day.

RUSSELL: No more houses of industry, no more Newgates, no more murderers on the bench, no more lackeys on the backstairs.

TONE: No more renegade Stuarts. No more Castlereaghs.

BUNTING: Ye think I don't want those things too? I do. But not your way, Harry, not your way. Have patience and ye'll see them all yet.

RUSSELL: Not by having patience.

NEILSON: It wasn't patience that pulled down the Bastille.

BUNTING: And what have they now? Two years of the Terror.

TONE: Ye read the wrong papers, Attie.

BUNTING: As a matter of fact, I do read Mr. Neilson's journal, Mr. Russell.

NEILSON: You are not among the subscribers, Attie. Will I take your name now?

MARY: Now, don't let this fritter away into badinage and banter. Edward was rather astute with what he said.

BUNTING: Thank ye, Mary.

HENRY JOY: Mary, we all love Attie. As a musician. But his politics—
ah, pah—you heard him yourself.

TONE: Bunting, I'm sorry but we're powerful bad listeners. Talk is
our native element.

NEILSON: And not talk only. But as a prelude to action.

TONE: Well said, O Jacobin. But I wasn't forgetting.

RUSSELL: Well, then, to get back to the music—Attie, don't you of
all men feel that these songs of ours are the melodies of slaves,
forever brooding on defeat and remembering someone brave
and dead—a long time dead?

BUNTING: And are they any the less lovely?

TONE: You're right there. Tragedy breeds the highest art.

HENRY JOY: Then I say away with it. Man's best state is in freedom
and content. That ought to yield and infuse the greatest music
and the best poetry.

BUNTING: But does it?

RUSSELL: I should exclude content and substitute wonder, wonder
at creation, its variety and magnificence.

HENRY JOY: So, the crystal and the daisy, the star ...

NEILSON: *The Northern Star.*

RUSSELL: But seriously, Harry, have ye never stood on a hill and
been lost in wonder at the pageantry of the night? Have ye
never risen above happiness and unhappiness with the pure
light of being. Happiness is in the full belly, the untroubled
nerves.

HENRY JOY: Tom, I have stood on a hill. So have you. And you. And
you. And that not a week ago. And we were out of ourselves,
part of a bigger thing, a glorious process in history.

NEILSON: The mount of transfiguration it was. I am a deeper man
for that day and that oath.

RUSSELL: But did ye not see the storm cloud over Knock and the
black shadows flashing out across the bay?

HENRY JOY: I saw them. And I saw O'Neill beside us and Sorely Boy
and—

MATILDA: And McMurrough?

TONE: Did I not charge ye never to speak of it?

MARY: Mr. Hutton.

RUSSELL: I shudder at the blasphemy.

HENRY JOY: Shudder me eye. We are rebels when we live for a

people and are Christians when we die for them.

MARY: Harry, don't talk of dying.

TONE: St. Jacobin, St. Danton ...

BUNTING: Ye'll all spoil Mr. Burton's next sermon for me.

HENRY JOY: I thought ye went asleep up there in the loft.

BUNTING: I do if the truth were told but not too soundly.

MARY: Do you remember the day one of the choirboys dropped a marble?

HENRY JOY: And the day your bonnet and mother's got entangled during prayer. I thought I would die.

MATILDA: Was it awful?

HENRY JOY: And when the congregation rose, Mary got a good firm grip of both of them and tore them apart like that—

TONE: What did old William do?

MARY: I don't think he saw us. I did it pretty quickly.

MATILDA: You see. It takes a woman to show resolution at a crisis.

RUSSELL: Mary, aren't ye going to offer us a glass?

MARY: I'll go fetch a bottle. Sally has gone out tonight. [*She rises and exits.*]

HENRY JOY: Good idea, Tom. I've got a fearful thirst. Not a drop since dinner. Mary would never think of it herself. She an ascetic.

MATILDA: Not ever sugar in her tea. I admire her.

TONE: I heard you went to see Hempson after the harp festival? I always thought Fanning was the best of them. And after him O'Neill.

BUNTING: Aye. As pure music you're right enough. But then Dennis was the only one who played in the old way.

TONE: I didn't notice that.

RUSSELL: But Theo, you should have. Long crooked nails to pluck the strings. And anyhow, think of it, he played before Charles Edward at Balmoral. That's a bridge across the years, that's history.

HENRY JOY: And your precious Charlie never spoke to him. He preferred the skirl of the pipes. Tom, you should make a squib about that. The 'Harper that played before Charlie, he came from over the Bann. The wind still shakes in his barley for he was the better man.'

MATILDA: Good for you Harry. Now Tom cap it.

RUSSELL: Sorry, Matilda, my spontaneous squibs take a while to
mature and no one could expect a man with appalling thirst to
speak immortal verse.

BUNTING: That going to see Old Hempson was one of the finest
moments of my days. Ye know he lives at the Down Hills near
Magilligan. There's the Bann with sandbank bleak and wild,
then the sheer cliffs of Innishowen over the water. To hear him
play in that place is beyond words. You only heard him sitting
up in a platform among the fine ladies and gentlemen. The
thing was wrong.

RUSSELL: Still, ye did get the tune for your book, Attie. And
otherwise they would be hard to come by.

BUNTING: Aye, indeed. I got material from everyone.

[*Enter* MARY *and* JAMES HOPE *hurriedly*]

MARY: Oh, listen everybody, here's Jamie and he's got some
important news.

TONE: The Spartan in person.

HOPE: Good night to ye all. Mr. McCracken and Mr. Tone, a word
with ye.

TONE: It's alright Jamie, speak up, you know everybody here.

NEILSON: It's not *The Star* or Mrs. Neilson?

HOPE: No, Mr. Neilson, not this time.

BUNTING: I think I'd better go. I haven't been sworn.

HENRY JOY: Sworn at plenty, I'll be bound ...

MARY: Harry, you're incorrigible.

HOPE: I was just leaving McCabe's a couple of hours ago when I was
accosted in Rosemary Street by a stranger.

NEILSON: Newell.

HOPE: No, Mr. Neilson, I know him. A stranger. A well-spoken man
who said he had business with me. Being on my guard and yet
not sure he wasn't from someone who's with us, I walked with
him to McDowells in North St. He called the drinks and talked
incessantly—first about the fine weather and then about the
United Men in a lower, secretive voice. He gave me to understand
he had something significant to communicate. When I pressed
him he parried awhile, suggested another drink and said all he
wanted was a wee list of the men I thought reliable, said he was
from Keogh and wanted it for verification and as a precaution
for a new line of activity Keogh premeditated.

MATILDA: Ye didn't give it to him? Keogh's in close touch with Theo.

MARY: Matilda, you don't know our Jamie.

HOPE: Thanks, Miss Mary. No, when I saw how the land lay I hedged a bit and said I hadn't my book with me but indicated that if he could give any credentials—

TONE: Oh, for a dozen of you, Jamie!

HOPE: He expanded then and crinkled notes in his pocket. The fool, the damned fool—as if I hadn't seen his game. I called the drinks then, gave him a hint we might do business ... The long and short of it was that I got him fuddled.

MARY: Did you hear that, utopers?

HOPE: And he got quite free with me, told me a lot of good stuff, to prove his good faith, mind ye, said that the number of delegates had aroused the worst suspicions of the authorities and they were for arresting Mr. Tone tomorrow.

MATILDA: Oh, Theo!

NEILSON: And us along with him?

HOPE: For they thought his continued stay here boded no good. But what he really wanted was an additional set of names of people to take up tomorrow.

HENRY JOY: They know about me.

RUSSELL: And they've been with me before.

HOPE: Yes, they know about you and you, Mr. Russell and Mr. Neilson. It was the others they wanted. Those they weren't sure about. A clean sweep. He misjudged me completely and fell for my trick. I suggested that if he could wait to the day after, I'd give him his list tomorrow night.

TONE: Good man, Jamie.

RUSSELL: Splendid.

HOPE: The fool didn't see I was playing him for delay and if Mr. Tone could get clear they wouldn't strike.

MARY: And do you think ye deceived him, Jamie?

HOPE: Completely, if I'm a judge of men. He went off unsteady to his employers and only with my promise to meet him tomorrow at ten. So, you see, there is no time to be lost.

TONE: I've been half expecting this. I knew we'd make him suspicious.

NEILSON: I fancy Cunningham's somewhere in this.

MATILDA: But Theo what are we to do?

MARY: Harry, what have you thought of?

HENRY JOY: I'm asking you, Mary.

MARY: Jamie, how does this seem to you? Mr. and Mrs. Tone to go home soon as if all were well. Pack immediately.

MATILDA: We are nearly packed as it is.

MARY: Good. I'll go fetch Dr. McDonnell in his coach. We could drive past the door about midnight. They can come out of the mews unobserved. It could be a sudden call out to the Limestones for the doctor, if anybody asked.

TONE: Would McDonnell do this?

MARY: I don't think you are fair, Theo. Dr. McDonnell has been a good friend. We found him a true friend, anyway.

BUNTING: And a musician too, Harry.

MARY: Then drive like the devil for Larne. We know where you could stay there.

TONE: And get a ship there.

HOPE: Or even wait for the American packet. Once you're away from here, they'll not make a move for they'll think ye really intended to leave Ireland. They'll be glad to see your heels.

MATILDA: Mary, Mary thank heavens your head's so clear.

MARY: Don't thank me, thank Jamie.

TONE: Spartan!

MARY: No flaws in that arrangement anybody?

BUNTING: If someone should stop the doctor—

MARY: James McDonnell won't be diverted when he's on an errand to save a life.

HENRY JOY: Good for you, sister!

NEILSON: I only hope McDonnell is at home. Perhaps some small infant is wailing his way into the world just at this moment or that some old rascal is screaming his last.

MARY: If I can't get him, I'll get his brother, Alexander.

RUSSELL: And in the event of—

MARY: If they're both away our last shot is McGladden, the apothecary—he bleeds and leeches himself.

HOPE: Has he a coach, Miss Mary?

MARY: If not, our own will do.

MATILDA: But I'm sure that the poor horses have had a fatiguing day.

HENRY JOY: Oh, they'll be rested alright by then.

TONE: Well then, it's settled. We can get to Liverpool from Larne and then get passage to the west easily enough.

HENRY JOY: I'm damned sorry this should occur. And on this day too.

MATILDA: Little we thought as we sported on Ram's Island and splashed each other on the way back that we'd be fugitives before another day. Thank heaven Mrs. Neilson did not have this shock.

NEILSON: Thank you for your thought for her.

RUSSELL: Might I suggest, it would call for less suspicion if I were to go for Dr. McDonnell.

MARY: No risk for me, Tom, at all.

RUSSELL: But Mary, it would call for no comment at all if I went. As a matter of fact, I do want to see him about a library matter. I could go now and warn him to be ready for midnight departure.

BUNTING: I hope you all trust me. You seem to have forgotten my unrevolutionary presence.

TONE: I'm right glad you're here, Attie. Lucky Devil—to witness a patriot's farewell in all its dignity.

HENRY JOY: Attie, to please me play us a song of parting and I'll never say music isn't queen of the arts.

BUNTING: I know a truly Irish tune appropriate to this regrettable occasion.

MATILDA: Do play it. 'Twill help us all.

[*Bunting plays* 'The Parting of Friends'.]

TONE: Come, your hand, Tom and yours Harry. Make a ring there, Jamie—and you too, Sam.

MARY: Matilda, this upsets me. I'm womanish enough to cry.

NEILSON: Attie, play it again. I remember its name now. It's called 'The Parting of Friends'.

BUNTING: I'm sorry, Mr. Neilson, I find it too affecting.

TONE: I hate rhetorical farewells. I can only say we shall—we must—meet here again in more auspicious times for Ireland. Though I go to the Americas with my dearest love and children my life is incomplete. I can frame no system of happiness for my future in which the enjoyment of Tom's society does not constitute a distinguishing feature.

RUSSELL: Tone, my friend.

MARY: Harry, you great goose, you're crying too.

HENRY JOY: A toast!

ALL: A toast!

TONE: Jamie, do you give it?

HOPE: Mistress Tone, Mr. Tone—The Temple of Liberty!—may each quarter of the globe supply a corner stone, may the canopy of the skies be its roof and may all mankind—all mankind—be its inhabitants.

SCENE 2

It is September 1797. The scene is Dr. James McDonnell's library and study, Donegall Place, Belfast. DR. MCDONNELL *is seated at writing table. Rap on door.*

MCDONNELL: Come in, whoever it is. [*Enter* JOHN TEMPLETON] Why, John, it's you. You're early afoot.

TEMPLETON: Not so early doctor, not so early. We out in the country are ever up betimes. It's you townsmen that are sleepabeds. I have already spent above an hour in the garden today. How are ye yourself man?

MCDONNELL: Rightly, thankee John, rightly.

TEMPLETON: And the others?

MCDONNELL: Oh Mrs. McDonnell's convalescing now—up a while in the afternoons. Alex is improving fast. The poor housekeeper is still the worst. By the way, you might sit down if you are in no hurry John.

TEMPLETON: You know doctor. I'm ever in a hurry betimes. I was afraid I would be taking up valuable moments from your patients.

MCDONNELL: Oh, I shan't be going round again for an hour or so. Do sit down. Here, John—oh leave the books on the side table.

TEMPLETON: I don't like saying it, for it sounds fulsome doctor, but you are a great man.

MCDONNELL: Nonsense, John—or should I say you are a great botanist, Mr. Templeton?

TEMPLETON: This turning over of your house to fever patients is one of the most—remarkable—er—humane—er—progressive ... that has happened in Ireland in my time. When there are so many would take life in this unfortunate country and hold humanity so lightly, it's a great man surely who gives his heart and substance to the alleviation of suffering and the healing of disease.

MCDONNELL: Oh, fiddlesticks. I can keep them here properly under observation—I don't need to go gallivanting around the highways and byways.

TEMPLETON: Oh, you'll still find time to go out and pick up a half-forgotten ballad in a lonely clachan or a new fossil in the quarry pits.

MCDONNELL: Aye, there'd need to be time for that or I would die of petrification of the brain.

TEMPLETON: Have you heard from Tom Russell recently?

MCDONNELL: Oh, Russell—no.

TEMPLETON: Oh, I was wondering—I had a letter yesterday. He's spitting blood. I thought perhaps he might have written to you about it.

MCDONNELL: Bad, that. I don't suppose he'll live to see fifty.

TEMPLETON: No, he won't, if he keeps as he has done—but doctor, we'll die snugly in our beds.

MCDONNELL: And the proper place too.

TEMPLETON: I wonder. A large number of highly significant persons have disdained that platitudinous conclusion.

MCDONNELL: Aye. Enoch for one. And how'd you like to be whisked away?

TEMPLETON: Doctor, you jest. You know well I do not accept that legend and you, as a scientific man, shouldn't even lend a facetious approbation to the story.

MCDONNELL: Come, John. Holy Writ, you know.

TEMPLETON: Simply, sir, my view is that the Almighty Creator would never use unnatural means for that which could be accomplished by natural.

MCDONNELL: And every thoughtful man would endorse your opinion. It is the only rational attitude. Still, I'm sorry Enoch upset you. The story has always delighted me. Mind pictures of the prophet's beard and hair flying as he was caught up or am I thinking of Elijah—it doesn't matter.

TEMPLETON: What I really called to see you about was the matter of the library. The fellow there now is not shaping too well. Being ill, you probably haven't noticed it. But we do need a change.

MCDONNELL: Aye. If only Russell had left politics alone. He was the right man for that work. Enthusiastic, cultured and versatile.

TEMPLETON: Yes. I miss him. You know, every time I catch myself daydreaming of the causeway or the tall cliff of Rathlin I get uncomfortably sad thinking of Tom and journeys we had together. Only this morning, I was inspecting my bank of heaths and I fell a-thinking of him. He was so enthusiastic about it every time he visited my garden.

MCDONNELL: Aye. The town's a duller place since they've gone. McCracken always had a joke or a scandalous story and Neilson was an earnest man—but tell me, how did you get on in London?

TEMPLETON: Fine, doctor. I went to the British Museum with those stones.

MCDONNELL: But what about Banks, I heard ye had an offer or something of that sort.

TEMPLETON: Yes, indeed. Sir Joseph's good works go on. A fine parcel of land and a considerable stipend—in the South Seas.

MCDONNELL: And ye didn't take it. Man alive, if I had a chance like that—

TEMPLETON: I would have been lost out there. No orchids for me. Just *rosa hibernica.* I'm really set on the Natural History of Ireland book. That's my province, my subject. Somehow, it's my life and my patriotism.

MCDONNELL: Still, I've heard you say the finest part of happiness was to unfold the volume of nature. And the South Seas are a brilliant chapter of that.

TEMPLETON: Yes, but a just evaluation of my meagre capacities and even the superficial survey of nature's scope, magnificence and variety, bids me be very modest in my ambitions. 'Irish Flora' will maybe be all I'll be vouchsafed as my share—if indeed so much. I become overwhelmed as my experience widens.

MCDONNELL: I know the sensation well. Just this morning, I was thinking of the harpers and their music and how I loved every air they played. And yet I'd give my right arm to be able to stamp out smallpox—yet that's why most of 'em were blind. And it's because they were blind they were taught to play. *So I am torn perpetually between the things I love and the things I want to see come to pass.*

TEMPLETON: My trouble is not from division of self into warring halves but stems from the sense of creation's sublimity and my insect-like worrying and concern, my petty scurrying here and

there, out under twigs and grass blades. That remark of yours
on the harpers reminds me. Russell was asking how Bunting's
Musick fared. And enclosed a tune for him he obtained from a
fellow prisoner. But I must be going doctor. I have delayed you
too long. [*Rap on the door*]

MCDONNELL: Come in there.

TEMPLETON: I must go. A patient perhaps.

[*Enter* MARY MCCRACKEN. MCDONNELL *rises.*]

TEMPLETON: Oh, good day, Mistress Mary.

MCDONNELL: Good morning, Mary. To what happy chance do we
owe this unexpected—

MARY: Oh, I'll soon let you know. Good day to you, Mr. Templeton.
I am pleased to see you here for I had thought a journey to
Orangefield unavoidable when I did so want to see you.

MCDONNELL: Is it orphans this time? Or sweep boys? The Sunday
school maybe? Or the charitable society?

MARY: None of them, doctor. It's more pressing business—about
Harry, Sam Neilson, Tom Russell.

TEMPLETON: I've just had a letter from Tom, Mary.

MARY: And the news? Good?

TEMPLETON: Fair. His health isn't too good. But his spirit is
magnificent. He sends Bunting a tune. He tells me of an
experiment he's done with a mouse in a chair of contaminated
air, discourses as well as ever on creation and its marvels.

MARY: And what else?

TEMPLETON: You didn't think I would forget the rest. No, I kept the
best to the last. He sends his regards to Bunting, to the doctor
here and asks that he be remembered to all that cared for him
and of course peculiar affection for yourself.

MARY: And no one else by name?

TEMPLETON: No, Mary, no one else.

MARY: I am content. I'm sorry his health's not good. He needs care
and attention so much but his heart was always high.

MCDONNELL: A great fellow, Mistress Mary, a great fellow. Pity he's
taken the revolutionary way. It can only end in defeat.

MARY: Not defeat. The time is ripening fast. I have had the most
encouraging reports from the colonelcies of the north.

MCDONNELL: Mary, are you Commander-in-Chief in the absence of
the others?

MARY: Not exactly. But I have means of communicating with those in prison and must naturally keep them informed of every detail.

TEMPLETON: How's Harry? And Willie?

MARY: Fine, impatient in captivity. They must feel so helpless cooped up in Kilmainham while everywhere throughout the province the tide of rebellion rises.

MCDONNELL: Mrs. Neilson tells me there is a coldness among them.

MARY: Ah, have you heard that too? It's a pity, a great pity. Ye see, at a time like this, everyone thinks of his and her own. Father, for instance, has been most anxious for Harry's and Willie's release but thinks Neilson's too extreme and could, with safety, be left to cool his heels. Poor Mrs. Neilson naturally thinks only of Samuel and the children's need of him. So she's been pulling strings and because of father and mother the Joys have been pulling strings to get this one released and that one. Then when the boys got to know they grew estranged a little. For Neilson has no relation so powerful as a counsellor. If they had the sense not to let the compulsory inactivity trouble their nerves they would see the situation in its proper perspective.

TEMPLETON: Oh, they must be distraught and over anxious. But I do hope they get understanding from experience. And, on their release, use their every influence, for the return of this distressful land to the ways of sanity.

MARY: It's about their release I called.

TEMPLETON: Is it imminent? Tom never once alluded to the probability.

MARY: No, it is not. That is, the declaration the government requires them to make is unthinkable. So James Hope and I have given serious and careful thought to the situation. We are agreed that if by some stroke of chance, Harry, Tom and Samuel Neilson could be freed to take control of the United organisation before it is too much impaired by spy and craven, they might be able to strike their blow and accomplish all they desire while yet the castle forces are unprepared.

TEMPLETON: Go on, Mary. I love a shapely plan.

MARY: Therefore, we must assist their escape.

TEMPLETON: But isn't Tom in Newgate while the others are in Kilmainham?

MARY: Aye. But fortunately I have heard from a friend that the authorities intend moving Tom over to join the others.

TEMPLETON: And playing into your hands! Bravo, Mary!

MARY: That will be, we believe, within a week's time. So the day after tomorrow, I leave for Dublin on business. I have to do a little buying for the winter season. My customers are already inquiring for the latest Dublin vogues.

MCDONNELL: John here's not long returned from London. He could tell you the fashions of the hour.

TEMPLETON: Doctor, your well meant diversion must be ignored. Your plan, Mary?

MARY: That part of it, I shall keep to myself.

MCDONNELL: Sorry, Miss Mary. I am sorry to have offended you.

MARY: James McDonnell, you have not offended me. I esteem you too highly, sir, for momentary levity to destroy my regard for a decade of service to Science and Art.

MCDONNELL: Thank you, Miss Mary.

TEMPLETON: But the plan, Mary. The part we are to be told of?

MARY: Briefly, I came here for the loan of money. If I draw any from my own bank I shall arouse suspicion—that is, any more than I usually take on a business journey. In order to bribe a certain jailer who has already been sounded for us and has been not unfavourable to the approach. I dare not ask the Joys in Dublin for there is one of their household whom I do not trust. So John I ask you for fifty pounds and you doctor for the same amount, if you can afford the loan. In security I offer the name of our house, Willow Wend, and the reputation of all its members for rectitude and honesty. To you, John Templeton, I offer security of the directorate of the Hibernian Republic.

TEMPLETON: Willingly taken on your own word, Mary. But you shall have to wait till this evening when I have visited my bankers. I do not carry so much money on my person.

MCDONNELL: Mistress Mary. You may think my obvious lack of enthusiasm for this cause determines my answer. That is not so. With my own recent illness and that of my wife, brother and the rest, I find myself unable to offer more than twenty pounds.

MARY: I understand, doctor. You have done much already for the cause of which you so sternly disapprove. That Mr. Tone is safe in the Americas is due solely to you.

MCDONNELL: That was nothing. Save a most enjoyable night drive, two-and-a-half years ago. Ochone, time flies. Another similar period, where shall we be?

MARY: Under an independent republic, I hope. United with France and America for the realisation of democracy and the rights of man.

TEMPLETON: Liberty, equality, brotherhood. Then doctor, I pursue my botany with a clear conscience.

MARY: And why not the doctor as minister for public health?

MCDONNELL: Mistress Mary, there has never been such an office anywhere.

MARY: But isn't it needed? Or does it take a mere woman to insist on the obvious?

TEMPLETON: And you, Mary? What office demands your attention?

MARY: I shall still attend my shop, John. That is after I have seen adequate legislation for chimney sweeps.

MCDONNELL: Funny, isn't it. Three unimportant little people in a small town dividing the world like Augustus and his partners.

MARY: Tomorrow then I shall call here, doctor, for your generous loan. Remember, please, it is that and you, John, will call on us later. I do not need to thank you. Let the thought of a blow struck against tyranny and bigotry be your immediate reward. Good day to ye both. No doctor, I found my way in, I'll find my way out. [*Exit*]

MCDONNELL: The amazon has gone.

TEMPLETON: A great woman, doctor.

MCDONNELL: I wonder you don't marry her, John.

TEMPLETON: I have thought of it—for there is not a woman in the town to compare with her for serious thought and energetic enterprise.

MCDONNELL: If she'd got an offer to go to the South Seas, she'd have gone and upset the world. Set Australasia in turmoil and the Islands in a blaze of democracy and rebellion. Phew!

TEMPLETON: Not while Ireland needed her. And Ireland needs me too in my own little way. But marry Mary! You forget she's set on Tom Russell.

MCDONNELL: Aye, and the scamp trifles with the affections of any woman but her. Even where his affection is not reciprocated. I'll bet you lied about the messages of love in his letter.

TEMPLETON: Not quite a lie. He wrote as I repeated but he added
  'you will know best to whom I would be remembered'.

MCDONNELL [*whistles*]: Miss Simms.

TEMPLETON: Aye, I think he meant her but little that hussy cares.

MCDONNELL: Did you tell her?

TEMPLETON: I did. And she only giggled—the bitch.

MCDONNELL: John, John you're losing your temper.

TEMPLETON: Who wouldn't? A good man, soul of honour, paladin,
  knight errant, wasting his golden affections on a light-headed
  slip of a girl who runs off after the next elegant ensign who
  struts down High Street.

MCDONNELL: Well, John, when your indignation has abated would
  you consider lending me twenty pounds?

SCENE 3

We are in the McCracken's home. It is 5th June 1798. Mary paces room restlessly. Peers out of windows, expectantly and dispiritedly. Sits down, rises and sounds below. Sits again for three or four minutes. Enter HOPE *and* HENRY JOY.

MARY: How did you find it?

HENRY JOY: Simms, he's betrayed us.

MARY: Oh my God!

HOPE: Not complete betrayal, Mistress Mary. Not active—passive, curse him.

MARY: Is all lost then?

HENRY JOY: No, my dear. Just as I went out I met Jamie here coming from Simms on his way to Dublin. Jamie had called on him for word of the turnout. Simms insisted he wanted instructions from headquarters, said he heard there was a rally of rebels at Dunboyne and gave him some money to go there and bring back his report. He further said he ordered the northern colonels to meet him.

HOPE: And I believed him.

HENRY JOY: I stopped Jamie at once; told him the truth, that there had been some fighting near Dunboyne but that the men had been defeated and scattered.

MARY: Yes, yes. I knew that.

HENRY JOY: So, deciding that Simms was either a coward or a traitor, we turned and went back to his house.

HOPE: He wouldn't see us but we forced our way in. He was stern with me at first, threatened arrest for my disobeying orders, but Harry was just as stern. We shouted him down and bullied him.

HENRY JOY: My God, he swore absolute innocence. I could almost laugh at his plight.

HOPE: Finally, he collapsed into his armchair and whimpered like a dog and his nerve was gone.

HENRY JOY: He did admit he got orders to call for the turnout on the 3rd, two days before that but had stuffed the message in his pocket and tried to forget about it.

MARY: And all this time the United men have been getting more and more impatient and letting rumour and perfidy and treason through their ranks.

HENRY JOY: Yes, that was his idea. If he held out long enough, all danger would have blown over.

MARY: We should never have trusted him when he withdrew from *The Northern Star.*

HOPE: I never did trust him. Nor, saving your presence, Harry, any leader of his class. 'Tis the people's own leaders must carry the day. Those Tone used to call 'That respectable class, the men of no Property.'

HENRY JOY: Right enough, Jamie.

MARY: Aye, but what else did you get from Simms?

HOPE: He resigned in favour of Steele Dickson.

MARY: Well, that's better.

HENRY JOY: Not when you've heard the rest.

HOPE: No, Mistress Mary. I ran round to John Hughes to inquire of Dickson's whereabouts and found he had been arrested last night.

MARY: What are we to do?

HOPE: Harry had stayed with Simms and when the fat old ruffian heard my news he blubbed afresh and forthwith appointed Harry general in his stead.

MARY: Oh, Harry, that's great. Now you can move at your own gait and to the devil with cowards.

HENRY JOY: We obviously can't call any more colonels' meetings.

HOPE: I don't trust one of them anyway.

HENRY JOY: So, I'll go write a proclamation. Jamie will run round to James Storey to print off a gross of copies and we'll get them sent out by trusty hands tonight.

MARY: We'll have to be careful. Half-an-hour ago, I saw Colonel Barber and some of the officers walking about in front of the exchange.

HOPE: Aye. And just now they were preparing to flog men in High Street.

MARY: Heavens! It's a mercy you weren't catched.

HENRY JOY: They might even be at this minute coming to arrest us.
[MARY *looks out of window.*]

MARY: Oh, Harry. There's a jostle of people in the street, like a fair day and military too. Mounted, bobbing up here and there.

HOPE: Have you any arms or powder here, Harry?

HENRY JOY: Aye, there's a bag below of musket balls and powder and a couple of swords and a green coat if anyone's wanting it.

MARY: Jamie, you'll wear it on the battle day.

HOPE: Devil a bit, Mistress Mary, any green coat for me. I've been a slave in these working clothes and I'll be a free man in them too. It's not coloured coats will win our battle for us.

MARY: I'd be happier if that bag was out of the house and in a safer place. There's little enough powder.

HENRY JOY: Ah, it's alright, Mary. If Jamie and I are taken, a bag of bullets won't make much difference one way or the other.

MARY: It's proof positive of your intent. Ye might cry innocence and stay out of their clutches. But with the swords and the coat—you'd be guilty beyond reprieve.

HOPE: Right, Mistress Mary. I always feel like obeying your every word for ye've a judgement I respect above any in this town. So I'll take it out.

MARY: Oh, Jamie, no. They don't all know me. I doubt of a single soldier has heard my name and I'll leave it with Charlie Scott.

HOPE: It's no more than a good stone's throw from here. But he's not suspected for he's been the soul of secrecy and his cart can take it out to the hills tomorrow on his way to Crumlin.

MARY: But Jamie if you're caught—we can't spare you.

HOPE: Och, there's many a weaver who'll be out with ye to Antrim. You'll not be missing me. I am a poor shot anyway.

HENRY JOY: No, Jamie. You are my right hand.

HOPE: Where's the bag? Harry, lad, will ye have the fighting orders ready for me to deliver when I come back.

HENRY JOY: Alright, Jamie. I will. Mary, show Jamie the bag.
[*Exit* MARY *and* HOPE. HENRY JOY *with paper and a quill sits to write.* MARY *returns.*]

MARY: Harry, Harry. Write the orders. I will keep watch on Jamie's journey. [*She goes to the window.* HENRY JOY *sits.*]

HENRY JOY: Report his progress, Mary, darling. I'll try to settle my brains for this composition is the hardest I've ever tried.

MARY: He's out now among the people. With the bag on his shoulder he looks like an old man. God, he's stopped—talking to a woman. They're laughing. He's gone on. Oh, he's saluting somebody across the street. I've lost him. No, there he is. He's at the corner. There's a knot of soldiers standing about. He's gone round out of sight. Heaven guard him. How's the writing, Harry?

HENRY JOY: Devilish hard, Mary darling.

MARY: Can I help you?

HENRY JOY: Oh, it's alright, Mary. You keep your eyes peeled for Jamie. He's more than a dozen fighting orders.

[*Silence.* MARY *stares at window.*]

HENRY JOY: Mary.

MARY: Yes, Harry.

HENRY JOY: I'm calling them to turn out the day after tomorrow.

MARY: The seventh!

HENRY JOY: Aye. Concentrate on Antrim, a county town. It's a convenient centre for us, for the Templepatrick, Doagh and Ballymena boys and for the companies from the Braid and from Toombe.

MARY: Will they get word in time?

HENRY JOY: Aye. They should, if Jamie comes back. He shouldn't be long now.

MARY: But it would be fatal if he showed too much haste. And what will you do after Antrim?

HENRY JOY: That depends on Antrim and the result. I'll send word to the Down Directory for a simultaneous rise there too.

MARY: Whose in charge now?

HENRY JOY: Harry Monro. If he's not been arrested.

MARY: Oh, Harry, Harry. I swear I can see Jamie. It's not—it is surely—aye, and taking his time too. Thank Heaven he's safe.

HENRY JOY: I knew he'd manage it. They'll never catch him. He's got no fear in him at all. And he's lucky. For fear is an admission, a concession to the foe. Most like me are a wee bit afeard and that makes the task all the harder for it gives the enemy a grip, even a wee one. But Jamie doesn't give it a chance. He's courage enough for both of us. And God knows we'll need it on the seventh of June.

SCENE 4

The scene is Colin Mountain. It is July 1798, immediately after the Battle of Antrim. The rebels are in flight. On the mountain are HENRY JOY MCCRACKEN, JAMIE HOPE, GEORGE DICKSON, *retired ex-soldier,* PAUL DOUGLAS, *his servant,* JOHN DICKEY, *Attorney of Randalstown,* JAMES ORR, JOHN STOREY, *printer of* The Northern Star.

HOPE: No sign of anybody coming?

DICKSON: Naebody at all, Jamie. I thought I saw the glinting of bayonets in the sun a while back over by Glenwhirry but I musta been mistook.

DOUGLAS: The silly fools—to signal their approach. If they only know to plunge their bayonets into the turf, they could make them dull. The time the Steel Boys wrecked Cunningham's huse we tuk that precaution.

ORR: It's damned few precautions we tuk at Antrim.

DOUGLAS: Aye, you're right. If only we'd had some of the Steel Boys but they're all near gone now.

HOPE: Aye, 'tis a pity. And if ye noticed it was mainly Defenders that was out and no United men.

STOREY: Now, Jamie, that's not quite correct. There was me and General McCracken and yerself and Captain Dickey.

HOPE: Aye, mabbe so. But I was a Defender and so was James here and Paul too for the matter of that. If we could have kept our ranks intact when we went over to the United we would have fared better. Wasn't all the leading officers in their hands? Answer me that now.

DOUGLAS: Aye, some.

HOPE: When fighting orders were sent, who sent them. McCracken. The general and Captain Dickey and Young Rab Wilson and mabbe two or three more but the others—

DOUGLAS: And even the gentlemen farmers weren't much better— Look at Sam Orr now, reneging and betraying like—

ORR: Robert Simms himself. Och, aye.

HOPE: It was sad to see that happen and till we have a body of men, of working-class antecedents and circumstances—

DOUGLAS: Weavers, Jamie.

HOPE: Aye. What's better? There's James now. And oul Nelson lying out there by the byrne. It's the loom does it. Working away, treadling and throwing the shuttle and your whole body completely employed, your mind winds free and ye get thinking hard and long. And then you're making something too. You're a producer. The farmer has only that at harvest. He's going on working on faith for most of the year but your producers— weavers and joiners and the like—ye see immediate material wealth at your hands made by you and it is then that you realise most clearly the gap there is between them that make and them that own and until we do and all working men do—and I'm not forgetting the farming laddies—ye might talk of the rights of man and liberty till yer black in the face.

STOREY: So, a Marat.

HOPE: Away with ye! That's no French. It's logic. Could ye ever see the Belfast merchants fighting for your rights until you have your own acre and cottage or—

ORR: Faith now, Jamie.

STOREY: But Jamie they were members of the union and good men among them—Mr. Neilson for one.

HOPE: Now, James Storey, ye know well, I excuse Neilson from this tirade. He was better than his class.

STOREY: You're always talking of class. Class this. Class that. Merchants. Workers. If you don't say it, ye think it. I've seen ye before this day and could tell and I not knowing who you were speaking to—whether he was a working man or a gentleman.

HOPE: How so?

STOREY: Oh, by your air. Your truculence to one and your good nature to the other. This forever setting up of classes will only breed trouble for Ireland in the future.

HOPE: I don't set them up. The gap is there.

STOREY: Oh, ye'll never budge. You and your class war. And now the gentlemen have had their touch, what about the working man? Where do you find them but in the Orange Lodges mustering agin us.

HOPE: Aye, you're right, God knows. But it's not their faults they haven't become—what's the word?—or is there one?—James Orr you affect a knowing of words—what's the word I want?

ORR: I see your point, Jamie. Let me see. Aye, conscious of their class.

HOPE: Glory be! That's it right enough. Class conscious!

[HENRY JOY *comes down with* DICKEY.]

HENRY JOY: I think it's time somebody went up to relieve George Dickson there.

HOPE: Right, Harry, I'll go.

HENRY JOY: No, Jamie. I'm reserving you for another job. Paul, will you go please?

DOUGLAS: Aye, General McCracken. [*He goes left and up.*]

HENRY JOY: Jamie, I want you to go over to the Killylane byrne and see if those two men are still there.

HOPE: Right Harry, I'll not be long. [*Exit* HOPE *to right*]

HENRY JOY [*to* DICKEY]: You know, James, we're damned lucky that all the grousers cleared off when we left Slemish. This eternal waiting would be intolerable if we weren't as good-humoured as a Sunday school class spending its Easter Monday on Divis.

DOUGLAS [*shouting*]: George, George Dickson! I want ye!

[DICKSON *turns alert and startled.*]

DICKSON: What is it Paul? Can ye see anybody?

DOUGLAS: Look there. There!

DICKSON: Oh, there. That's nothing but an old fella at his work. I seen him this hour or more but you're a good chap, Paul. It tuk me a quare while to sort the whole landscape out. The trees, the clachans, the bastes in the nearer fields.

DOUGLAS: Alright, thanks George. I'm sorry I brung you up. I hate to be crying wolf.

[DICKSON *comes down again.*]

DICKEY: This is a grand place for seeing the countryside now.

HENRY JOY: Aye. And we've seen a good bit of it since we climbed the mote at Donegore.

DICKEY: And we'll be seeing a lot more before were done, I'm thinking.

HENRY JOY: Aye, Slemish. It's the far cry from old Patrick to us.

DICKEY: I mind thon epigram ye made there.

HENRY JOY: Which one?

DICKEY: The one about Slemish is an extinct volcano. So's St. Patrick.

HENRY JOY: Oh, that. I'd forgot. I'd be remembered for something better than that I hope.

DICKEY: It does seem a bit flat out there now. But, when you said it, Slemish was rising in front of us like a great black shadowy cone and we were all distraught and upset by the nervous wreck of battle. I know I blessed you for that laugh you gave me. For a minute I was able to forget the deserters running off here and there, the silly gibbering of frightened men, the horrible jolting and discharges of guns, the sickness of defeat and misery of hopelessness. I laughed and I said to myself, 'There's Harry McCracken. He hasn't lost heart. He hasn't faltered. He's going on. By God I'll go on too.' And so here we are.

HENRY JOY: Thanks, James. Ye know you're the first lawyer I ever respected or liked?

DICKEY: What about the councillor?

HENRY JOY: Oh, him. Formidable my dear chap, formidable. But he did get Willie and me out of Kilmainham when Mary's bribery went astray.

DICKEY: So, some lawyers are of use.

HENRY JOY: Aye, there are so many of them that they can't all be wrong all the time.

DICKEY: Well, there Lucius McNally. He's lost a lot through supporting the Union, and defending prisoners for little reward or fee and getting a whale of criticism from the bench.

HENRY JOY: I met him in Dublin and, in spite of his good record, I don't trust him. As a matter of fact it was Jamie Hope who first planted the seeds of doubt in my mind about him. Sorry George, our chatter wasn't helping you to get to sleep.

DICKSON: It's all right, general.

HENRY JOY: General yourself. You earned the title. I was only nominated to it. James, you must be a grand democrat, it's damned few masters and men marched out together for liberty.

DICKEY: And I'm thinking he's the better man—I certainly wouldn't have risked disarming those five fencibles and we retreating too and the battle over. I think not.

DICKSON: Aye, Mr. Dickey. But I'd funked stabbing the traitor Sam

Parker and you had to do the job instead like a stern Roman of the old story.

HENRY JOY: There's a subject for ye, James Orr. A classic tale in brazen couplets!

ORR: General McCracken the last month has given me more subjects than I have time tae write aboot if I lived till I was a hundred.

STOREY: There *is* a subject you'll not need to bother with.

ORR: What's that?

STOREY: Victory. You'll not need to give that an ode.

HENRY JOY: Storey, you're a croaker! We're confounded lucky to have a poet with us to immortalise us and make us part of Ulster's lore forever by his craft.

DICKEY: You forget, Harry, James Orr's a fifty pounder himself and unless he's careful not to be catched there'll be a sharp end to all his songs.

ORR: Now you're all talking Bardic Rhapsodies and whatnot. Would ye like to hear what a real poet longs for most at this hour?

HENRY JOY: One guess is sufficient. I need a drink myself and not spring water either.

DOUGLAS: General McCracken, general! I can see someone coming.

HENRY JOY: Where, Paul?

DOUGLAS: There, general. There's only one.

HENRY JOY: It's a woman. Good heavens—it's Mary. [*Waves to her*] She sees where we are.

DICKEY: It's been a week since we saw her last. How can she have found our hiding place?

HENRY JOY: Och, it's better known than we think. I'm sure every step we've taken since we left Slemish has been noted and marked down.

STOREY: Mr. McCracken, we shall have to look out for a new territory for I think we've been on everyone of these hills in our time. [*He points.*]

DICKEY: We just crossed that.

STOREY: Glenhead. Carnmoney. And here.

HENRY JOY: There's Shane's Hill to the east there. That's in the direction we want to go now. Over the bog hill.

STOREY: Mr. McCracken, have ye given up completely your plan of working east and south and joining the Wexford boys?

HENRY JOY: I have. And what new plan will replace it depends on my sister here.

DICKEY: You see, James, striking south after making a detour of Belfast was all very well when we had fifty men or so but with half-a-dozen we'd be no accession of strength to any group.

STOREY: Aye, and we might have a terrible journey. As it is, we aren't so bad for the time being.

DOUGLAS: Miss McCracken, General.

HENRY JOY: Right O.

[*Enter* MARY]

MARY: Oh, hullo, Harry. You're looking ill.

HENRY JOY [*hugging her*]: And how's everybody?

MARY: Everybody? Well to begin with mother's well but worried. Father's much the same but I've noticed him walking with a martial tread as if he were with you in fancy, Harry me lad. Willie has got to the coast.

HENRY JOY: Oh, thank heaven! I've been worried about him. Not seeing him after Antrim and not hearing a single word. And Frank?

MARY: Francis is safe.

HENRY JOY: Grand.

MARY: But not stirring about much. The military are wild, rampaging and roaring about the countryside. Poor Mrs. Hyndman was stripped and flogged. There's been a tremendous row about that. They mistook her for a working woman or a servant girl. The rumour has it they'll be forced to withdraw. You boys are more popular now than ever before. If you'd only waited until the people were rightly disgusted and roused, you'd have a different story to tell this day.

HENRY JOY: Mary, let's not go over that again. We moved when we decided and here we are. I am content. It was a mistake but not our mistake. There was treachery but not our treachery. There was cowardice but not among us. It is for historians to figure out. We are no more than pawns laid at the side of the board.

MARY: Harry, I'm sorry. I didn't want to rouse you to any bitterness or grief at all. Here in this parcel are some clean shirts, some hose, a dozen bannocks and farls, a couple of pounds of butter and some tobacco.

HENRY JOY: Mary, you're a goodness from above. Here, James Orr, will you open this bundle and lay out the contents for our vision?

ORR: Right, General.

STOREY: If you excuse my butting in, Mistress Mary, but have you heard of Mr. Neilson?

MARY: Yes, Mr. Storey, I have. Mr. Neilson is in safekeeping now. He's lying a prisoner in chains on a boat.

STOREY: Thankee, mam. And Mrs. Neilson?

MARY: Poor Mrs. Neilson is prostrate. Doctor McDonnell has been very kind to her in her trouble.

DICKEY: No good, Mistress Mary, me asking if my folks—

MARY: Captain Dickey, sir, I'm sorry but I've had no information at all from Crumlin and you, James Orr, aren't very far from home yourself.

ORR: No, Mary, but there's many a stile and sheugh to be traversed still.

MARY: Paul Douglas, Paul Douglas.

DOUGLAS: Aye, aye, mistress Mary.

MARY: I saw your wife and she's well and happy to know you are safe. She's sent a pair of socks for ye. I have them here in my bag.

DOUGLAS: Thankee, Miss Mary, thankee and gae my bonny sweetheart all my love.

MARY: I will, Paul, I will.

HENRY JOY: Mary, how on earth did you manage to get here this day? It's sixteen miles or more to Belfast.

MARY: I came by road as far as Ballynure. And I walked from there.

DICKEY: That's at least four miles, Miss Mary.

MARY: Three and a half. I should explain that John Templeton has come out with me. Botanism, you know.

HENRY JOY: Sly dog, where is he?

MARY: Oh, he didn't come right up here. He's scratching about a mile or so down the hill.

HENRY JOY: Did he funk coming up?

MARY: Harry, you're not fair to John. He's been a great help and strength to me in these troublesome days. Oh, in many little ways. Already the military have taken a dislike to him.

HENRY JOY: Well, he is good company.

MARY: He's been visited by Colonel Barber and asked point blank has he seen you or Captain Dickey here or any of the others. So, he insists on being in a position, should that inquiry be made again, of complete truth in denial—that's why he's grubbing about in a ditch a mile from here. Having driven me here from town and carried my bag most of the way from the coach.

HENRY JOY: That's like him, Mary, but I'd wish he'd been with us all along and turned out with us.

MARY: No, Harry. John Templeton will shed no blood. He's adamant about that but he's a fearless and honest man and a true friend of Tom's.

HENRY JOY: Oh, Mary, Mary. Why did ye mention him? The lack of him and his military skill and strategic genius has been so oppressing my spirits that I've tried to shut him out of my mind. With Tom Russell we could have snuffed out Nugent and his army, turned south, joined with Monro and turned Saintfield and Ballinahinch into victories like Valley Forge and Bunker Hill. Oh Tom, Tom we needed you, and we are needing you still.

MARY: I'm sorry, Harry, but I've lain awake and brooded over the same loss. If only ye had Tom Russell's experience and energy. George Dickson, I expect you know that you are on the list of fifty pounders and you too James Orr.

ORR: Fifty pounds for me. There was an English poet once ransomed for sixteen pounds. They'd give fifty pounds for my head—a lock of money for a hundred poems mabbe and one wee treasonable thought.

DICKEY: That means now, Miss Mary, that Hope's the only one without a price on him—that's damned odd.

MARY: It is so but Jamie has been discreet, even in waging actual warfare.

ORR: But he was in the front rank with the Templepatrick men.

MARY: Oh, they must know him but it's an oversight he's not on the list or else they don't think a Roughfort weaver of any importance.

ORR: Well Miss Mary, I'm a Ballycarry weaver myself.

HENRY JOY: I fancy it's for economic reasons. There are things that are priceless and unobtainable. They know they'll never catch Jamie Hope, so why put the price on him. I'm glad to think I'm worth as much as a poet.

MARY: Now Harry a word with you myself. You don't mind Captain Dickey or James Storey? [*To* HENRY JOY, *privately*] Harry, I didn't want to be too pessimistic before the others but I can be frank with you. The fight is over. It wasn't much at the best. A scramble here and a skirmish there. No matter whose fault— the United Irishmen are finished, smashed, wiped-out. Now all's left is for you is to save your skins, each for himself. I've got a pass here for you and one for Captain Dickey and there's a peddler's pass so one of the men can have it. I'll give you them now. You can give Dickey's later to himself. It's a pity that I couldn't get enough to go round and it wouldn't be fair to make a choice among them. Let them draw lots for it. These will get you past any military or yeomanry patrols, if you're not identified. But you mustn't waste much time. I suggest you head for Islandmagee. Once you get to Scotland, on a smuggler's cutter mabbe, you could be pretty safe. You know Scotland—

HENRY JOY: Only once there, my dear.

MARY: Oh, well, you could pass among them easy enough. Be an Ulster linen merchant. You could play that part.

HENRY JOY: To the life, Mary. But I need money.

MARY: Yes, I've got some here. And some for Dickey. And a little for the others but your best safety lies in scattering and going about singly. The only parties on the move of any size are loyalist Crown forces and government ruffians, so scatter, I tell you. I can't keep on slipping out to find you. It won't always be as easy as today. And if I were followed and you were taken, I'd never forgive my foolish judgement. So, Harry, this is really goodbye.

HENRY JOY: Mary.

MARY: Now, Harry, no movement or affectionate gesture. We must not alarm the others unduly. When I'm gone you can hold council, ballot the peddlers pass, divide the money and scatter on your ways. Scotland and then America I suggest and mabbe you'll have a quieter life there among more merciful and juster men for only among such could you be at peace.

HENRY JOY: Do ye remember how I said once we all come back to Ireland by every road we take?

MARY: I do that, Harry. I mind the time and place. Well mabbe you will come back to Ireland in ten or fifteen years' time. Willie's at the coast already I told ye. He won't have much difficulty in making his escape. You'll have him for a companion in the United States and some one of father's cronies might take me with them on a tobacco journey sometime.

HENRY JOY: I suppose there's nothing left to be done. I did want to link up with the Wexford boys.

MARY: No chance of reaching them, Harry. The country between is hiving with yeomanry and dragoons. Tell me, was it true that Dickson here captured five fencibiles?

HENRY JOY: Och aye, and disarmed them and chased them like rabbits all on his own.

MARY: They say in town that Paul Douglas is a deadly shot.

HENRY JOY: Aye, he picked off half-a-dozen at Antrim like snipe.

MARY: Well they should all be fairly well able to look after themselves.

DOUGLAS: General McCracken, General McCracken. I see someone approaching. Seems like Jamie Hope, sir. There's someone smaller with him. A child, sir.

MARY: Oh, I'm glad. I wanted to see Jamie before you all cleared off.

DICKSON: I wonder whose the wee lad is? A houl ye a shilling James, it's from your missus to tell ye it's twins this time.

ORR: It must be you, James. I'm not married.

STOREY: Nonsense. My wife wasn't expecting.

DICKEY: I wonder has he left the two still at the byrne.

MARY: What other two?

HENRY JOY: Major and Burns. I don't think you saw them. We have them lying out in that direction as a kind of outpost. Their view takes in a large slice of country we can't rightly overlook from here.

MARY: Heavens but you've dwindled.

HENRY JOY: Aye. A couple of hundred at Donegore, then about fifty, rising to eight on Slemish as the Ballymena fugitives came in. Now there's only nine of us and maybe only seven.

MARY: Do ye think the two you named might have gone off?

HENRY JOY: Aye, good luck to them.

DOUGLAS: Here's Hope now, sir.

[*Enter* HOPE *and* BOY]

HOPE: Back again general.

HENRY JOY: And who's your captive?

HOPE: Oh, hullo, Miss Mary. I'm glad to see you.

MARY: Good day, Jamie. I'm happy to see you still hale and hearty.

HOPE: I suppose you've had a budget of news for everyone.

MARY: Yes. And I did see Rose, Jamie. Or rather she came to see me. She bids you be brave and don't worry. Luke's well and thriving.

HOPE: God bless her and you too, Miss Mary. You're the two best wimmin in the whole world. Excuse me, Miss Mary, I must make my report. General McCracken, I went to the byrne and failed to find the outpost. I searched about but they'd gone and left no rag or stick. It's my belief they decided to try their luck in the dark and went off. They are both men from this countryside and could easily get back among friends.

HENRY JOY: I don't really blame them but it's damned bad for discipline. Half one's army deciding to go home, and going home without so much as whistling goodbye to their general. But the boy, Jamie, the boy.

HOPE: I came upon him soon after I left the byrne on my way back. He asked me if I knew how far it was to where the rebels lay. I was careful but he's an honest lad. His da was out with the Keady men but got back home safe. So, I brought him along. Let him deliver his message himself.

BOY: If you please General McCracken, I come from Mr. Magill, Mr. John Magill, whose daughter is married to John Bankhead, the minister, to tell ye that he's heard the clergyman at Ballycaster has informed your whereabouts to the soljers at Carrick and demanded that ye be cleared off the mountains for ye've lain here too long and Mr. Magill told me to tell ye that he'd advise ye to get clear this day or this night but no later.

HENRY JOY: Thanks, sonny, you're the brave lad. Pity we hadn't had you with us before. It's boys like you we needed and still need.

BOY: Oh, General McCracken, I know a fair deal.

HENRY JOY: What do you know?

BOY: I know U—

HENRY JOY [*laughs*]: I know N.

BOY: I know I.

HENRY JOY: I know T.

BOY: I know E.

HENRY JOY: That's fine. What do you bear in your hand?

BOY: A green bough.

HOPE: General McCracken, time is going very rapidly

HENRY JOY: It's alright Jamie. I was having a bit of fun. But I suppose it's over now. What do you say, boy?

BOY: Yes, general.

HENRY JOY: Aye, the bough is withering I'm afraid. Mary, have you a sixpenny piece for this hero?

MARY: Aye, here you are.

BOY: No, thankee mam.

HENRY JOY: Oh, a Spartan too!

BOY: Please sir, I don't know what a Spartan is but Mr. Magill—he gave me a florin to come here, sir.

HENRY JOY: Well anyhow here's a sixpence. You needn't spend it. Keep it to remind ye of a brave thing you once did for rebels and outlawed men.

MARY: Well, Harry, I'd better be going myself. So maybe this lad could guide me down easier than I came up.

HENRY JOY: Will you, my boyo. Right then.

BOY: Yes, general.

HENRY JOY: Right then. Goodbye Mary. Thanks for the clean shirts and remember me to mother and father and the others when you see them.

MARY: Good day to ye all. Any that I may encounter who ought to hear from you I will acquaint with your best regards and affection. I shall see you all again I am sure.

HOPE and DICKSON: Thank you, Miss Mary.

HENRY JOY: Paul, have you any message for Miss Mary to take to town?

DOUGLAS: Oh, tell my beauty not to let the soljers buzz round her too much. Their bite is poisonous.

MARY: Alright, Paul. I shan't forget. It is the advice she'll be needing with her looks and graces.

STOREY: Good day, Miss McCracken. And don't forget to tell all who'd like to know that the general was grand at Antrim and has been magnificent ever since. Tell your father, tell your mother.

HENRY JOY: James Storey, you're a blether.

DICKEY: Good day, Mistress Mary. In more prosperous times I should have sought an assignation with you but for the present good day.

MARY: My cavalier, oh there you are. Lead me up, lead on, fair sir.

BOY: Yes, mam. [*Exit* MARY *and* BOY]

DICKEY: Harry, you ought to go part of the way down.

HENRY JOY: No, James. I shan't be so affected if I stay among you. Goodbye, Mary.

MARY [*distant*]: Goodbye.

HOPE: Now for a council instanter.

HENRY JOY: Aye, tell Paul there to take a good scally round and then come down for he's in this too. [HOPE *goes.*] Captain Dickey, your map please. [DICKEY *draws it forth.*] Oh, James. Hand out a few of those farls. I'm famished. George, wake up. Here is a bit. Paul, soda or wheaten?

ORR: I wish Miss Mary had included a bottle.

HENRY JOY: Not her—dislike of liquor is her only weakness. Jamie, you can slip up to the outlook now and see that we are not disturbed. Captain Dickey, would you kindly show us just where we are and how to get out of it.

SCENE 5

As in Scene 1. It is 18th July 1798, immediately after the hanging of HENRY
JOY MCCRACKEN.

BUNTING: Come in, Mr. Templeton.

TEMPLETON: Good day, Doctor. I hope I don't intrude upon your
studies.

BUNTING: Studies, bah. In this house and at this time?

TEMPLETON: I thought perhaps the grief had given inspiration—

BUNTING: Sorry, Mr. Templeton. I'm overwrought and irritable
but with all this day's going on and our great grief it's a wonder
anybody's sane around here.

TEMPLETON: Mistress Mary. How is she?

BUNTING: Excellent. She bears up and has seen to everything. Mrs.
McCracken is prostrate, poor woman, and Mr. McCracken is
sitting in his room unapproachable. He's been ill, you know.

TEMPLETON: God help them all.

BUNTING: While Mary has seen to everything—

TEMPLETON: Is she resting now?

BUNTING: No, she's down below with the body.

TEMPLETON: I thought they'd taken it to Barclays.

BUNTING: No, Mary prevailed. Alex McDonnell is with him now,
trying his skill.

TEMPLETON: With any hope of success?

BUNTING: That I can't say. I fear not. Though there were those at
the execution who thought by the slack hanging Harry would
have a chance.

TEMPLETON: Poor chance Dickey got, I hear.

BUNTING: Oh, you weren't there then?

TEMPLETON: I was for a while, I saw Dickson's struggle, pitiful that.
I could endure no more. So I left and went to call on Dr. James
McDonnell.

BUNTING: Aye. And did ye find him in?

TEMPLETON: No, I must confess. He'd gone to the country and might not be back today—

BUNTING: Ye know why, I presume?

TEMPLETON: The doctor's natural caution maybe.

BUNTING: Fiddlesticks, sir. Funk—that's what is was. Yesterday, Miss Mary called and asked him to come round today after the hanging to try resuscitation. She'd been to the military and by cajoling and threat had obtained permission to have Harry's body without decapitation.

TEMPLETON: Aye, I heard that. I wonder how she made her point.

BUNTING: God knows. She'd get any point. But McDonnell promised last night but now today he's fled. His brother came over in his stead.

TEMPLETON: James McDonnell has disappointed me several times.

BUNTING: He's failed me too before now and he certainly didn't play fair by Tom Russell.

TEMPLETON: I know. I was deeply distressed by that.

BUNTING: That's what comes of running with the hare and hunting with the hounds. No wonder Mr. Tone calls him the hypocrite. Mind you, I gave Harry McCracken less support for his militant projects than any of his acquaintance.

TEMPLETON: Yes, I've heard you even oppose him strenuously.

BUNTING: Aye, I believed he was wrong and was I not right? But that doesn't matter. I detest folk saying smugly 'I told you so'. I thought him wrong but here I am and here I'll stay as long as Miss Mary needs any assistance I can give. Though I don't suppose a poor music teacher could have had as urgent a call as a physician. Mr. Templeton, sir, you yourself are no fair-weather friend. Witness your coming here today at this hour—

TEMPLETON: Tush, doctor. I think you're a trifle hard on McDonnell though. His heart's in his hospital and if he can get the wealthier members of his community to back him he'll do great things for the diseased of all classes. Suppose they got wind of his sympathy for the United men. They'd drop him like a shot. And the hospital with it. He's taking a long view, Dr. Bunting, a long view. We must not misunderstand him.

BUNTING: The wealthier members—Simms and his brother, they themselves were once United men and you know rightly how they betrayed their trust.

TEMPLETON: I suspect you, Doctor Bunting, I suspect you of not being so antagonistic to the Union as you protest.

BUNTING: You're wrong, Mr. Templeton, but I like honesty and consistency in all things. If you haven't that, what have you? And when a man puts his hand to the plough, he shouldn't draw back even if it is a lonely furrow itself.

TEMPLETON: We're a pair of old wives, Bunting, gossiping here, tittle-tattle, bad word of this one and that one, comfortable only in our own virtue while Harry McCracken is lying downstairs dead, dead for his dream and a row of heads are on the spikes that were on good shoulders today.

BUNTING: Aye, Mr. Templeton, but somehow a time like this gives one a truer perspective of men and events and there's many that will have a black name from this day through all eternity.

TEMPLETON: And by the same token, there are those who will be among the immortals.

[*Enter* MARY]

BUNTING: Oh, Mary, what's the tidings?

MARY: Oh, John, it was a kindly act you coming here.

TEMPLETON: No, Miss Mary. I was a friend of Harry and yours. And I came to see what a friend might do this day.

MARY: Thank you, John. Attie, it's all over. Harry's dead. They could do nothing. Alexander McDonnell did his best but it was useless.

BUNTING: I'm sorry Miss Mary. And your hopes were so high.

MARY: Why else should we hope?

TEMPLETON: You must be weary, Miss Mary. Can you rest? Can McDonnell give you a draught?

MARY: I cannot rest. There is much to do. No one else to attend to it. You know Harry's to be buried at once.

TEMPLETON: My God, no. They'll let you keep him until tomorrow or the day after.

MARY: No, John. The general has just sent an order that the funeral must take place immediately or they will take Harry from us.

BUNTING: What can I do Mary? The coffin?

MARY: The girl has seen to that. It has been ready since six o'clock.

BUNTING: The grave? Is it opened?

MARY: Word was sent. He is to be laid in the family ground.

BUNTING: Shall I go and supervise? See if all's well and decently done?

MARY: Aye, Edward if you would.

BUNTING: Willingly. [*Exit* BUNTING]

TEMPLETON: Miss Mary, you must rest.

MARY: No, John. My nerves are set to carry me through the day. I can endure it but what the reaction will be I know not but I can go on. I did not sleep last night and early this morning I was with Harry and we spoke wisely and quietly of his death but do you know when I wanted a lock of his hair and the young officer had got me scissors, Fox came in and rested it from me crying there were to be no more relics of martyrs in this God-damned land. Harry bade me not to resist him, so I surrendered it but I have got a lock of it that I will preserve despite the crowd of foxes.

TEMPLETON: I heard you were with him to the end. I had thought to remain myself.

MARY: You were there though. God bless you, John.

TEMPLETON: I was for a while but Dickson's double strangling was too much. I retired.

MARY: Merciful God, I didn't see that. I came out with Harry when Dickey and Storey were despatched. Harry asked me to go at sight of the scaffold but I clung to him and stayed. It was then that I wept first. He commanded me to the care of Mr. Boyd who led me away. And after Mr. Armstrong conducted me home.

TEMPLETON: I was told that Harry stood and watched after you until you were out of sight and he then tried to speak to the people but the noise of the horses and the roar of the crowd was so great that what he said was not heard. On an occasion like this words are inadequate. I cannot say the things that are in my heart. Before the magnitude of your grief I am abashed. And I prided myself on my philosophy, on my stoic unconcern.

MARY: Your views are close to mine I warrant. Our lives are in the hands of God. It is His will. He has called Harry away. This then must be the fitting moment though it is wrapped in mystery.

TEMPLETON: If that comforts, Miss Mary, believe. Providence has seemed plausible in my study, in my rock-garden and on the hills but my wits are baffled before the shadowy approach of the last enemy.

MARY: Tush! Must I indicate God's ways to you, who have touched
the hems of splendour in many a place?

[*Enter* ALEX MCDONNELL]

ALEX MCDONNELL: Miss Mary, we are ready. The men are here. And
they wait your word to bear him out.

MARY: I am ready, Dr. McDonnell.

TEMPLETON: My arm, Miss Mary, lean upon it for the stairs are steep
and the passage narrow.

MARY: Do you know John, he was hanged on the parcel of ground
that his great-great-grandfather gave the town.

SCENE 6

*The McCrackens' drawing room, as in Scene 1. It is the winter of 1845.
Enter* SERVANT *first. Then* HOPE *and* MADDEN.

SERVANT: Come right in, Mr. Hope, and you too, sir.

HOPE: And Miss Mary, is she well?

SERVANT: Aye, sir, very well indeed but resting you know resting in
her room. I'll go wake her.

MADDEN: Oh no, don't please. Let her finish her nap. We can wait.
Our business is not urgent.

HOPE: Faith, no. It's waited near fifty years and if it wasn't for you
doctor, it would still be waiting.

MADDEN: Do go an' leave us. We'll be alright. Call Miss Mary at her
usual time and let her know we're here.

SERVANT: Yes, sir and she won't be long for she's been lying down
this half hour, thankee sir.

[HOPE *sits.* MADDEN *faces room, looking at pictures.*]

MADDEN: This is Harry, I suppose?

HOPE: Aye, a fair likeness too, just a bit effeminate though and
Harry wasn't that.

MADDEN: And is this William or Francis?

HOPE: Francis about the same time. A great old man. He only died
a year or so back, you may remember. The ranks are thinning
fast. Francis was the last of the Belfast volunteers. It seems
strange that. I can mind easily the parades for the fall of the
Bastille. The banners and the drums, the uniforms, the prancing
horses and shouting men and now the last of them's gone. And
France has had another revolution

MADDEN: Aye, it seems to go just like that. We are forever greeting
the new day but it never quite reaches our expectations. This
one's Russell.

HOPE: Thomas Russell. The truest of the brave. A great man, a
good man.

MADDEN [*sitting down*]: You know, I've been giving most of my time and thought to the recapturing of the spirit of those days. I've read this pamphlet or that manifesto, I've talked to this one and that one, I've gone out about the roads and lanes, I've walked this day in the rain over Donegore Hill among the sycamores. There have been moments when I have felt this was it. Just this. A man's face by firelight, the slope of a mountain, an unexpected name above a shop and in my heart there was of a sudden a touching of permanence, a realisation that they and I, McCracken, Russell, Neilson, walked together with no gap between. Jamie, I envy your perpetual exaltation. You knew these men intimately, their slightest gestures were familiar, their lightest tones remembered and what I gather by intuition and imaginative effort at rare intervals is yours by inalienable right. You have proved by unflinching loyalty to those men while they were alive and to ideals when they were dead that you have the right to rank with the champions and heroes of the annals.

HOPE: Now, Dr. Madden, you're waxing rhetorical. It was simpler than that, I joined the Union in the springtime of its strength from a conscientious conviction of its principles being right and having no reason to change my opinion of the advocates of these principles went down before the murderers in high places and I was bound to that cause to which I had pledged my life. Force may yet prevail for a time but there is music in the sound of moral persuasion which will be heard like the sound of the cuckoo. She lays her eggs and leaves them for a while but they will be hatched unwittingly and at strange places and the song will return with the season.

MADDEN: Rhetoric, Jamie, no—but poetry. [*Piano plays*] There's someone playing in the house.

HOPE: Aye, it's Miss Mary's niece. She bides with her and the old lady likes the company.

MADDEN: I hardly realise she is old—remember I've never met her. Her letters are extremely legible and unfaltering in their penmanship. I always think of her as young and eager, busy here and there, tireless.

HOPE: Aye, as when she came to us in the bog hill or out to Knockbracken in the dark but you see I've watched her grow old as I grew old and as Rose grew old, God rest her, the two best women in the whole world. Dr. Madden, Miss Mary has not changed in spirit, I needn't be telling. A little deaf maybe and maybe troubled with her eyes but clear in her mind as a spring well.

SERVANT: Miss Mary is up now and is coming down straight away. She scolded me for not wakening her.

[*Enter* MARY. *They rise.*]

MARY: Good day to ye, Jamie. And is this Doctor Madden?

MADDEN: At your service, mam.

HOPE: You'll have to speak a bit louder, doctor.

MADDEN: At your service, madam.

MARY: Good day doctor to ye, doctor. I'm right glad to see ye. Only why didn't ye let me know you were calling and I wouldn't have been dozing upstairs like a lazy old tabby cat. I'd have entertained you as well as I might. Though we are poor these days and it's little cheer there is in this house for a hearty man.

MADDEN: It's alright, mam. It's only by chance we thought of calling. Today, that is. I have promised myself the happiness and privilege of meeting yourself someday. You see, I happened to be with Jamie going over the ground to get places and times fixed in my mind for my work.

MARY: Your work, Doctor Madden, a great work surely. And gratifying to an old woman with a failing memory.

HOPE: A great work truly. You know, Miss Mary, the doctor has done a deal among the freed slaves of the Indies. His passion for justice has got him into bother before this.

MADDEN: Come, come, Jamie.

HOPE: Aye, it is so. And it was no chance occurrence that a baby born during a raid on his father's house in the summer of '98 and a young man bringing mercy to the oppressed should take up the task of rescuing the memories of valiant men from the infamous histories of privileged cupidity.

MARY: Doctor Madden, Jamie and me, thankee ye heartily for all your labour and research. It was not a work either of us was fitted for and yet it had to be done if men were to profit by the experience of some of the best intellects this land has given birth to. Before you began doctor, I used to think sadly of the waste of it all. Harry and Tom and Sam Neilson, giving their lives for an ideal and that ideal being dragged into the gutter. And their sacrifice rendered vain. Now I am well content. The Lord has sent his scribe and the tablets shall not be erased.

MADDEN: You are kind, mam. It is little that I do and I cannot help doing. The inspiration of meeting Jamie here and now you will keep me ever assiduous and untiring, the heritage of honourable memory is one of man's greatest treasures. And it is but common duty not to let the laurels vanish as the lights go out.

MARY: Nicely expressed, doctor. The heritage is in safe hands.

HOPE: The doctor and I went to Donegore this day. We climbed the long hill to the mote and as we stood on the height I pointed out the place where we arrested Mr. Adair, the magistrate, Lough Neagh grey beneath the winter sky, Carnmoney where Tom Russell went to rouse the men, wee Colin where we heard the guns of Ballinahinch. It makes you sad Miss Mary, so long ago.

MARY: Aye, Jamie, sad. There's scarce a day when I'm not sad. I go to my ragged school. I attend charitable society meetings, I visit the fever hospital, I am busy over many things, like Martha, but I cannae forget. And this room too, Jamie, don't you remember?

HOPE: I do. Dr. Madden it was in this room that I brought word for Mr. Tone to fly. [*Piano plays* 'Let Erin Remember'.] Harry was here and Sam Neilson and Mrs. Tone and Miss Mary here and I fancy Dr. Bunting. Am I right, Miss Mary?

MARY: Who?

HOPE: And Dr. Bunting.

MARY: Aye, you're right enough.

MADDEN: I'm sorry we bring back such bitter memories and uncover such old hurts.

MARY: It is right that you should. By pain the spirit lives.

HOPE: Come now, Miss Mary, there is joy in it too and hope. This island moves on. Already the old hates wither between Catholic and Protestant, already a juster conception of patriotism spreads its beneficent power and when Dr. Madden writes his book, the hearts of men will leap up and they will become aware of the glory that was and the splendour that shall be. Good will and peace to all men and none to make them afraid.

[*They are silent. The piano plays on slowly.* HOPE *laughs.*]

MADDEN: What are you laughing at, Jamie?

HOPE: I'm thinking, doctor, of the days ahead when we have come into our own ...

MADDEN: A worthy hope Jamie—but why laugh?

HOPE: They'll be having coats in the museum we never wore and swords we never drew and maybe pictures of us, cheek by jowl, with better men.

MADDEN: Not better, Jamie.

HOPE: Well, maybe people painted better. William Nixon did me only a year or so ago. And I'm not very pleased with the result. It's a sour fellow he's made me.

MARY: It'll be a horrible revenge if your spirit walked the shining corridors only to find your face framed close against Waddle Cunningham the land usurper, a would-be slave trader

HOPE: If they are wise enough and kindly enough to have pictures of us, they'll be of Harry and Tom, Sam Neilson and maybe Mr. McCabe but never of Cunningham and others of his breed.

Curtain

THE ANGRY DOVE

A Verse Chronicle of the life of St. Columcille

VOICES
in order of appearance

Axall
Demal
Ethne
Female Voice
Florence
Boy
Finnian
Bishop
Brendan
Columcille
Monk A
Monk B
Monk C
High King
Molaish
Conan
Dermaid
Canice
Comgall
King
Druid
Hag
Aidan
Counsellor
Queen
Crimen
Herald
Dallan Forgael
Mochonna

[*Opening in outer space with vast wind rhythms in background.* AXALL *and* DEMAL *speak on echo.*]

AXALL: You're waited for, my friend and enemy;
we two have one more clash of arms to try;
another skirmish in the vast campaign
before day breaks in Hell and once again
your master and your draggled fellows come,
sick of rebellion, to our Father's home.

DEMAL: My master's pride at yours must veil his face;
you name who'll win before we start the race,
and claim the outcome certain, tho' by now
Hell's roaring legions, mustered row on row,
outnumber and outflank your dwindling clan.
There's not a sin that cannot choose its man,
and set him running eager to our ranks,
and if you'd stop him you'd get little thanks,
for all the heart desires is on our side,
the answer to its lust for power and pride.
We've fought this same ground over once or twice,
but I'll not quarrel with the loaded dice.

AXALL: So you must spin your logic to the end.
I wait you still, my enemy and friend.

DEMAL: Then tell me, on what errand are we joined?
What time and place that chance has thrust and quoined
in the dark temple of eternity?
[*A rushing sound during descent to Earth: then, maybe, suggestions of evening birdsong, lowing cattle, falling water.*]

AXALL: We drop from sphere to sphere, until the sea
breaks on the cliffs along a little land
where Europe ends and time runs dark and slow,
where small and warlike kings an instant stand,
awed into silence at the overthrow
of their, and your, dark idols at the hand
of one, blest Patrick, who has torched the Light

75

across the waters to their pagan night.

There is a manchild born but three days since
whose father, Felim, is a northern prince,
and we are bid to try with love or hate
that infant-soul, and shape him to his fate,
for he's a soul unplumbed, of strength and power,
a small clenched bud that may achieve the flower
of sanctity, or yield its honey'd heart
to swarms of maggots which could rise and start
a gale of wrath and storming violence
to blight his fair land like a pestilence.
Come, see below the shoulder of that cloud
on the June sunshine of a windy glen,
there lies the clan-encampment gay and proud
with tiny flags and coloured tents of men.
DEMAL: So like a game; a neat and painted toy—
    no ten years' tedium this of one more Troy.
AXALL: Now closer yet. The largest tent's our place.
    The prince since morning following the chase,
    sits weary now, his brown hand carelessly
    stroking the hound's long muzzle on his knee.
    The mother, Ethne, speaks low-voiced, for fear
    of waking the small man-child cradled near.
ETHNE: O Felim, I have had a terrible dream
    in the grey dawnlight after you had risen.
    A figure stood before me with a robe,
    a King's robe, more than a King's robe, wrought in gold,
    and shook and spread it solemnly, and then
    let the wind's breath, that lapped its broidered skirts,
    lift from her grasp and billow it away,
    and as it rose and broadened like a tent,
    I cried out for the loss. The woman spoke—
    she was a woman, comely as my mother—
VOICE [*on echo, female*]: Let you be happy. This robe is for your
        son.
    You cannot hold it. His bright destiny
    is to be blessed by half the waiting world.
    This was, and is, the garment of his grace

that moves with mercy over the rough hills
and over the grey waters to other shores.
He is your son. You must surrender him
to time and place beyond your care.
You must wait and know
the abject glory of the lonely mother,
whose son's name fills the broad world's lip,
while she still stirs the pot.
And should his high fame stilt him up with pride,
there'll be a tempter waiting. His name is Demal;
but on the other side good Axall stands,
a holy angel, one of the never fallen,
to urge and beckon, to bind the ragged wounds
that the bad Demal must inflict him with.

ETHNE: Thus prophesied the woman in my dream.
O Felim, I had hoped for easy days.
I'd thought our houses had been surfeited
with violence, and that our sleeping child
had smoothly walked a temperate friendly road
with quiet wisdom to a peaceable end.
But that was folly, for I should have known
that any prince of your great Clan O'Neill,
born in this rocky quarter, could not fail
to find his war and weapon anywhere.
Pray with me then his war be in the right,
whatever field it fall in, and he keep
God's bright Red Hand before him all his days.

AXALL: So we are named and planted in this play,
white against black, the yea against the nay
to wring a consummation from the fray:
not a mere end and final, but a force
for good or evil, that will take its course
throughout the ages following and be
an element in all eternity:
a soul's fate certain, but far more than that,
a warning beacon or an open gate,
a strong wind blowing towards the shores of truth.

DEMAL: Or sharp example of the claw or tooth.
But take him, he is yours now. For my part,

with the old evil on his human heart,
he's halfroads mine, will need not to be taught
the ready lie, the calculating thought
the lusting sense, the single selfishness,
the clumsy hand that wounds when it would bless.

AXALL: I take your offer. I shall have him set
with a good man to learn the alphabet,
not of script only, but of wrong and right
that he may learn his destiny aright,
know what's expected from a prince's son.
Stand by and watch him. Let the swift years run.

[*Music rising and fading to a tolling bell. Then a rising babble of children's voices.*]

VOICES: Church pigeon, church pigeon, wouldn't come out to
            play,
Church pigeon will your eggs be hatched soon?

BOY: I'm no church pigeon. You shouldn't shout at me.
If I go after you I'll pay you back.
Florence, they shouldn't call me names like this.

FLORENCE [*male*]: You must be patient, child. Their shouting
            names
won't hurt you—you are not the same as they:
you're of a different breed. Your blood is hot
with the fierce temper of your father's race,
and if you once let go, you'd go too far.

BOY: If I'm a prince's son and a warrior's—
you should not order me like a whelp—
to crouch to insult.

FLORENCE: That's the blood I fear.
Your father's house were fighters; your mother's kin
lift even now the tallest Leinster spears.
Your being patient is a victory
beyond their reach: and greater victory
if you should take that name that they throw at you,
and wear it like a brooch upon your cloak;
not jerking pigeon strutting on the tiles,
but great white Dove whose prayer and thought have power
to offer wings of shelter to the world,
because men know you have the eagle's strength

    but not his cruel heart. Dove of the Church.
BOY: I do not like the name. It is too timid,
    and how should I appear among my house?
    My father's brothers earn new battle praise,
    their sons, their cousins, play with sword and sling
    and talk of spear throw and the hurling field.
    Yet I must walk among them slow and grave
    who could outthrow them were they twice as tall.
FLORENCE: Aye boy, you could. You know. I know. God knows.
    Let that suffice. You cannot see a boy
    but you must shut your fists and charge at him.
    God knows your quality. He'd make of it
    a keystone for his arch. He knows your worth;
    why else has He so gravely tempted you
    with such a rash inheritance?
    and further set against you, to draw you up
    to your full height of character, a demon,
    a tempting demon, one of the fallen angels,
    that you should win, not merely assume the crown.
BOY: A demon? What is this? My house I know;
    their acts and courage now are balladry,
    but this strange tempter?
FLORENCE: I should not have spoken,
    but let you find the knowledge for yourself.
    This always is my way. I say too much
    like a bad teacher who must spoil his lesson
    by offering more than the small hands can cup.
BOY: You should not. But you have. Now you must tell.
FLORENCE: This demon, this bad angel, is called Demal.
    He took the ring against you from the first.
DEMAL: We are reported, marked, but will he learn
    the trip, the sidestep, and the sudden turn
    we thread through like a dance we know too well
    that might yet win him Heaven or end in Hell?
AXALL: When Florence tutored him to read and spell
    my purpose led him where the grave monks dwell
    at far Moville, the Plain of the old tree
    where famed St. Finnian ruled in sanctity.
    Where the long lough is spattered with green isles

at height of tide, and where for dreary miles
that tide runs hissing from the tufted mud:
in that bare land the famous college stood.
There the grave dove, Columba, ground his wit
on scripture-scholarship till he was fit
to argue doctrine with the wisest men;
but that the hard-wrought meanings be not lost
he laboured at the parchment and the pen,
till of the Irish scribes, a noble host,
he had few masters with a defter hand,
and both his skills grew known throughout the land,
till who was pupil, who was master there,
became a hard opinion to declare.
And reaching manhood all remarked his sense,
his rooted knowledge and his diligence,
his harnessed strength, his force of mind and voice,
the beadroll of his blessings and his joys,
the ascending promise of his princely race
bright in the beauty of his gentle face.

DEMAL: I too endured that promise, and the threat
of striding sainthood, unachieved as yet,
his lengthening shadow cast. The turbulence
that veins the people of the rocky glens
beat in his fists and flickered in his glance.
I watched his power give leash to arrogance
and saw hope there, that mustered on my side
the anger of his fathers and their pride,
the constant chafing of his leaping heart
against the monk's coarse vesture, as apart
from his strong kin who stormed from feud to strife,
he paced the flagstones of monastic life.
I knew my man. I knew the break would come
and lucky wind and tide blow up the foam.
His master Finnian was a haughty priest,
swift to discern rebellion in its least,
quick flicker, and resenting it, to press
against a heedless youth's hot eagerness.
Columba now intent on winning grace
by wilful effort, overstepped his place,

his junior station in his master's house,
the temper of St. Finnian to arouse,
who, feeling his authority at bay,
sent out the word and summoned on a day
a conclave of his peers to ratify
the duty owed to that authority,
and prove to the young upstart how his sin
of mortal pride, through his indiscipline,
struck at the Church, and by what swift degrees
would wreck the architecture of God's Peace.

I waited, watching, gently whispering,
my quiet little barbs to fret and sting
the ready heart to rise in revolt,
and as the black cleg will urge the pawing colt
to leap the traces, smash the bounding fence,
and break his own heart with his violence.

The solemn fathers gathered to debate
the young man's errors, and deliberate
on what were fitting punishment for these,
should such be proved. Yet for his greater ease
in compassing his aim, sly Finnian ran,
bestowing where he could on every man,
the hint, the nod, the whisper and the word
obliquely uttered, rather overheard
than offered at the bar of evidence
where truth might blast it in its brisk defence.
[*Fade-up babble of crowd, fading a little as* FINNIAN *speaks*]
FINNIAN: Look. Columcille approaches. His proud step will lose
　　its vigour when he hears our judgement.
BISHOP: But his kin are princes; he'd whip and drive us
　　to his unruly will. He thinks his right
　　admits defiance to his superiors ...
　　this thundering deacon, this roaring dove of the Church ...
　　[*Crowd assents*]
BRENDAN: You are too harsh. You overlook his youth.
　　You once had fire when you were young as he.
　　[*Crowd protests*]

Have you forgotten? We have not heard him speak
his own defence yet. Let your sentence wait.
[*Crowd disagreeing among themselves*]
FINNIAN: His face is set in that stern pious mask
the choirboys shrink from. He will not find us
so easily cowed. [*Shouts of assent*]
BISHOP: Look at his poor garments
so ostentatious in his poverty. [*Sneering voices*]
FINNIAN: Face him with silence, all.
COLUMCILLE: Good day, my reverend fathers. I have come
to answer for my actions, and await
your sentence, Master.
FINNIAN: With humility? [*Laughter in crowd*]
BRENDAN: Finnian, you should not vex him. Columcille,
my greeting. [*Crowd expresses surprise*]
My dear son, I bid you welcome.
FINNIAN: Brendan, you forget. You prejudge his case
by being so affectionate. He stands
on trial here before these witnesses.
[*Crowd assents*]
You know his slight on me [*Voices 'Aye, Aye.'*]
Yet you must set this evidence at naught
and meet him like a brother. [*Voices accuse BOY*]
COLUMCILLE: He does but greet me—
BRENDAN: My Columcille, no more. Your eager tongue
has bred its mischief. Brendan shall speak for you
My reverend fathers, you have blamed my act:
I gave you this. Our brother may be bold,
even unruly, surely indiscreet— [*Crowd laughter*]
This is the force, the liveliness of his faith.
Are you so old and groomes in aisle and stall
that you forget that Lord Jesus brought a sword?
I would not have the brother otherwise.
Did you not see, as I saw, when he came here,
the shining angel who accompanied him,
bright evidence of his young innocence
your threats would sully? Could you not feel
the very air grow warm with benevolence?
I'd rather take my stand by what I know

than lean on the oath of a man with a tender hide—
FINNIAN: —Brendan, you are unfair—
BRENDAN: —who points to a blank weal of imagined hurt.
   He has my vote, tho' little needing it.
   [*Applause: 'Brendan is right,' etc. Cross-fade to Demal's signature tune close behind.*]
DEMAL: The meddling Brendan baulked me. My device
   for breeding hatred as the eggs of flies
   will hatch in fevers and putridities
   of general infection, failed for once
   though I have kept it handy ever since
   for when I need it to smear a good man's name
   no other method earns so little blame,
   and I can point to more than one strong town,
   that I have brought in ruin down.

   So baulked and thwarted, to my master bid,
   I crouched before Him, and in terror hid
   my hurt face from His lashing outraged thought
   that roared round Hell till demons were distraught,
   and licked my spirit in its searing flame
   till, coupled with His wrath, my wrath became
   a terrible plague that ran across the land
   striking its thousands, blotching tongue and hand,
   with the black spittle of its fearful rage,
   and like a war that fabulous Titans wage
   death ran through th' Abbeys and the villages
   that clustered round them, till like winter trees
   stripped of their leaves, the beams and rafters thrust,
   disthatched and black against the barren sky,
   as the plague whipped along the rutted dust,
   and kine unmilked ran madly out to die.

   For our hot anger grew so terrible
   that not a hut or cabin where men dwell
   but had its shrivelled starveling stiff and dead
   across the hearthstone or the tumbled bed,
   and those who still could stir limped hollow-eyed
   to plunge their screaming fevers in the tide,

and pestilence swept over beasts and men
as the grey mist swarms down the darkening glen.

But my stark target slipped me; like one who trod
across the glowing turves unscathed he strode
yet half in panic, turning to his home
in the rough northland where the salted wind
blew clearly in and fresh, that he might find
a haven where contagion had not come.

AXALL: Weary and heavy-hearted he came back
ragged and weeping, by the mountain track
mourning the unhoused relic, and his book
ripped by the gales, its leather case unstuck.
But sun and sea restored him, and secure,
with love about him now no longer poor,
in the small hills beside the shining Foyle
he found his strength again in friendly toil
and built his hut at Derry, Place of Oaks,
Derry forever darling of his heart,
where, with slow thunder of the woodman's strokes,
the tall trees turned to walls of simple art,
and there, because he found his fate his choice,
the high roof arches the echo of his voice,
and men drew in to labour, and a town
of fishermen and farmers settled down
close to his shadow, safe beside his name.
Here joiner, mason, thatcher, blacksmith came
and consecrated their strong artistry,
in service bound and so in spirit free,
till Derry of the Oaks, a lodestone was
that turned both love and labour to his cause,
and gave a name to time that must outdate
the troubled years of courage and of hate.

DEMAL: Remember Derry. I have found that place
an easy tilt-ring suited to my pace.
Men at my bidding, since Columba's time
have packed its story with transcendant crime,
slaughtered the hostage and betrayed their kin
and lived by hatred like a discipline.

AXALL: That story's still to tell, and tell in truth,
    not in the jargon of the polling booth.

    I speak of wise Columba whose scant fare
    set an example few had strength to share,
    for close devotion and humility,
    bowing his proud heart down obediently
    in prayer and daily labour at the mill,
    in meditation, and the penman's skill,
    and ceaseless thought for strangers; everyday
    checking his urgent tongue, that longed to play
    with the fine curves of rhetoric, to words
    that paid the small coin of companionship
    without the bitter wit—and bitten lip,
    till free in worship he outsang the birds.

    I summon for my proof the men that strove
    to match their labour to his restless love.
MONK A [*a rough voice*]: Yet he would often slip beyond the walls
    and in his easy stride come to the shore
    where the loved waters break with foam and weed
    on the smooth rocks, and there he'll scramble up
    an overhanging cliff and watch the stars
    die out with the dawn, save the one morning star
    that waits till the first shadows rib the dew,
    in silent meditation, never sleeping,
    but armouring his soul against the day
    and its bright tempter colours.
MONK B: Once he touched
    the clenched crab-apples on a wizen branch,
    and bid us eat them—they were clean and sweet,
    pear-sweet and dripping cider round our lips:
    yet he would not taste one, altho' we urged.
MONK C: Derry he loves, but most he loves the trees,
    the wide oaks spreading. We would cut our names
    in the rough hide; his gentle word forbids it.
    He will not suffer an axe on a growing limb.
    Even when the great wind from the clouded west
    lifts up and throws them down, or when with age

they lurch and topple over, nine long days
must pass, by his order, before we dare take them,
and then the work is numbered; a third is drawn
as fuel for the guest-house, and a tenth
scored off and measured for the poor, the rest
is piled, and tied, and carted to be given
freely to those who work at forge or quarry.
For Derry thrives and grows, and needs their labour.

AXALL: And hear him singing to himself alone
the proud Columba, Felim's princely son,
Columba, 'Dove', by childish nickname still
tagged 'of the Church', forever Columcille—
who knew not only how to copy out
the crabbed scribble of scholastic thought,
but like the bards in Eire well could trace
his lilting lyric in the margin's space. [*Music*]

COLUMCILLE: Were all mine the breadth of Scotland,
from green centre to grey shore,
I would rather have in Derry
the oaktrees at my door.

This is why I love my Derry:
for its kindliness and peace;
for the singing crowds of angels
thronging white in every place.

This is why I love my Derry
for its peace and charity;
shining bright with little angels
is the leaf of every tree.

Little oakgrove, lovely Derry,
where I built my narrow home
God above, if one should harm it,
let Thy wrath descend on him.

Little oakgrove, lovely Derry,
where I built my narrow home ... [*Fading*]

DEMAL: This Derry idyll was too good to last

all out of character, a sunbeam cast
between his heart's black storms. I played and played
upon the strung nerves tethered to a trade
that could not long be his. I set my snare
and he rushed at it as a hurley player
leaps at the puck. In Teffa, in Drumfin,
where fortune led him from his place and kin
he found a parchment Derry lacked, a skin
close-lettered with a subtle commentary
dusty upon a shelf, the property
of his former quarrel master, Finnian,
who now wrought here, an unforgiving man.
The scribe's lust seizing Columcille, he longed
to copy it, yet scarcely had the heart
to beg permission whence that right belonged,
but spread his clean scroll out and made a start.

I set the stage: on the right, the scribbling monk
tonguing his lip, intent, his strong chin sunk
on his broad chest, and urging his slow pen
to match the eager hurry of his eye
ending the sheet before the inks are dry
along the scroll-top. Finnian enters then,
there in the lefthand shadow; shafted sun
falls evening level, mellow golden on
the knuckles and the tonsure of the bowed
unresting scribe, his pots of colour set
before him on the desk. The two are met
a silent moment. Finnian speaks out loud.
FINNIAN [*approaches*]: What, Columcille, not gone to evensong?
    Eking the last light out? It pleases me
    that you should labour so for one who cannot
    lay claim to a close place beside your heart.
COLUMCILLE: For you, good Finnian? Say rather for the brothers
    who back in Derry need this book.
FINNIAN: They still must need it; for the book is mine
    I was not asked leave to copy it.
COLUMCILLE: Not yours in truth. You do not own this copy.
    You have the stained original. What I make

goes back with me to Derry when I go.

FINNIAN: You have no right to take it: the words are stolen,
  they still belong to me. I will not lend them.

COLUMCILLE: Lend, Finnian, lend! By the right of my right hand
  these characters I've written are my own.
  You do not need this copy. You cannot read
  two books together with an eye on each.
  I scraped the skin and sized it and made the colours,
  and copied out the lines. Skin, inks and hand,
  all these are mine, and what they make together
  can be no less than mine—
  I sand it now and roll it carefully.

FINNIAN: Come, give it me.

COLUMCILLE: By God, I will not. For this second affront—
  for you are always out to master me—
  Since Brendan saved me from your jealous will.
  I'll go to the High King now, and ask his ruling—
  not ask—demand—for there can be no doubt
  in such an issue. That will silence you.

FINNIAN: Not silence, Columcille, but satisfy,
  with his good ruling that I still am right.
  Come, to the High King then. I do not fear him.
  [*Fade-up accelerating music—cross-fade to murmur of crowd*]

COLUMCILLE: Your judgement, King. I have heard the arguments
  in patient silence, repeated tediously
  till they have lost what little force they had
  in this stiff lawyer's gabble. [*Crowds protest*]
  I am an urgent man
  and do not like this jargon. I want to know
  whether I keep this copy I have made,
  or whether Finnian steals my sweat and skill
  to add another unread parchment to his shelves.

FINNIAN: High King, I beg protection from this brawler.
  [*Crowds agree with* FINNIAN]

HIGH KING: You, Columcille, but weaken your case with temper;
  you should be reverent to Finnian. [*Crowd assenting*]
  He was your master once and ranks above you.
  [*Crowd assenting*]
  I say this object goes to him who holds

the mother-manuscript, the original.
The calf goes with the cow till someone buys it.
And Columcille offers no purchase for this calf.
Here, I deliver it to Finnian's hand. [*Crowd applaud*]

COLUMCILLE: If this is what you rule in flat defiance
of all the crowded sense upon my side
that I have tried to reason out in words
not even a King should fail to understand
I will not take it. There's a higher judgement
which heeds or heeds not opinionated monarchs
according as the terrible wisdom of God
gives edge and fury to the whirling blade.
My house is not a hall of sycophants,
but warrior's lodge of strong and angry men.
I shall but rouse them to the wrong you've done me,
and place the issue on their dagger points.
[*Uproar from crowd cross-fading into the rolling of drums; hold drums
behind.*]

DEMAL: Then I was loosed upon the quaking land
till little flickering spites were quickly refined
into a general blaze. The northern lords
itching for a cause, took up his words,
and drove against the High King. War began
there at Cooldrevny, where the ditches ran
with blood, and the King's people scattering
were harried into Connacht. Heath and ling
were raked and prodded for the hiding men.
Then at Coleraine the King's host rose again
and struck the rebels; at the monarch's side
the stubborn Finnian prayed, but like the tide,
white-horsed and crowding up the crumbling banks,
Columba, charging with the foremost ranks,
bade Michael the Archangel lend his aid
to the long spear-thrust and the whirling blade,
and no cry in the tumult rose above
the terrible anger of the raging Dove.

AXALL: He would not heed my whisper in his heart;
the rage was on him from the very start,
and unabated ran its headlong course,

for who can dam the torrent at its source
when that's among the clouds and out of reach?
His ear was stopped to any pleading speech,
so great the press about him, as he hurled
his shouting cohorts on th'astonished world.

DEMAL: Then famine crawled the roads in battle's tide,
the uncut corn was fired, the children died,
and Autumn saw no harvest, and the frost
lay, ember smirched, on the year's labour lost,
and Winter knew no comfortable feast,
no rest for man, no fodder for his beast.
So when the war dragged sullenly till spring
and they should go a-ploughing, languishing,
sickly and weary, both sides sheathed their swords,
shamefaced at such a gale begot by words,
and turned to build the walls their rage had wrecked,
but Columcille, discountenanced, deject,
stood blamed by both and cursed his thoughtless crime,
waiting the sentence of an outraged time.
I worked against him still to rouse the land
that he be driven outcast, every hand
lifted against him, and no longer one
that men might heed and follow as a prince's son;
till all the muttered anger made its choice
out of the clamour, of a single voice,
the voice of sage Molaish, of holy men
the oldest, most revered, and duly then,
armed with opinion, bold with sanctity,
Molaish faced Columcille in urgency.

MOLAISH: So, Columcille, your mad acts now have brought
destruction over Ireland and its folk
because of your pride and insolence, thousands have
suffered
innocent of your hurt or name. I command
that you go from this country, never again
to see your native landskip while you live.
I cannot sever you from our Mother Church;
your early works, the witness of the Saints
speak for you. Go, and in some other place

labour by mercy to wipe out the stain,
as much as in you lies, altho' you cannot,
by any miracle encompass all.
Three days to muster friends—if you have such—
and victuals for them and shipping. Then, depart.
And never look again upon Irish ground,
exiled from her, not alone
by my weak voice, but by the united will
of God and Man provoked to finality.
[*Fade-up music—seafaring theme.*]

CONAN: Master, master, it's time that we went on board;
the seamen are uneasy, the tide runs fast.

COLUMCILLE: Be patient, Conan, there still is time to spare.
Would you, my friend, grudge me this final hour?

CONAN: The midnight bell has sounded; the cables strain:
the ship is eager for the light brimmed sea.
Already the Captain murmurs anxiously,
for he has purposed by broad noon to steer
thro' Carrickmeckan and its spinning crests;
and, if you idle here, we'll be overtaken
in the coil and trouble of Rathlin's meeting tides
by the black moonless hour. Master, let us go.

COLUMCILLE: My sentence said tomorrow. Can I not wait
till the first cockcrow call the yawning light,
and I can spend my last gaze on Inishowen
wearing the shrouded gold on his highest peaks,
and see the dawn wind ripple the Foyle's grey reeds?

CONAN: We'll still be inshore for a league at least.
You'll hear the cockcrow off Magilligan strand,
and still have your Irish daybreak to remember.

COLUMCILLE: Perhaps, my Conan, if I saw and heard again
the brown larks rising, and the tide of light
breaking in foam of song from field to field,
I should, in my soft nature, break my penance,
and tempt a worse end than the wide horizon.
Conan, I come. The course is to the East.
[*Up seafaring theme and fade-out slowly*]

DEMAL: I could rejoice. My victim driven out,
disgraced, despised, and utterly in rout,

to vex and trouble with his rabid grace
some other people—and some other place,
his shining reputation and his deeds
spattered with malice, choked with rapid weeds.
Yet I'd not finished with him, for my task
was his defeat and capture. But I'd ask
no better fortune than to have him tossed,
disheartened among strangers, frustrated, lost;
for in that plight he'd be a swifter prey,
a flame by night, a cloud of smoke by day.
Exiles fall easy in the tempter's snare,
the fresh seductions of the foreign air,
or clinging to the fading dream behind,
unchecked by fact, assume a brooding mind
prone to infections, lacking the old pride
that kept him pacing with his kinsmen's stride.
From now I'd be content to watch him rot,
his wrongs remembered and his joys forgot,
to fall when ripe into my waiting hand,
leaving a tale to his tormented land,
one hero more whose self-accomplished end
betrayed the cause he laboured to defend.

AXALL: Others have made their epics of that flight,
begun at cockcrow, bringing holy light
to those that dwelt in darkness heretofore
by many a rocky firth and craggy shore.
But let the words of one, his servitor,
bear that brave curragh through the whirl and stir
of the grey floods that race by Rathlin's Isle;
he tells the story in his simple style,
as though he plied a ferry to and fro
on some smooth inland river drifting slow,
and had not set mere osiers and hide
against the terrors of the toppling tide.

DERMAID: When we pulled out a league we hoisted sail
and cleared the sandy Bann mouth; Rathlin then
came up ahead and passed us on the starboard.
The Moyle was kindly, crossing to Kintyre,
where Conal dwelt,

the King of Dalriada, a Christian prince.
He welcomed Columcille and would have stayed him;
but our good master spoke his earnest wish
to find an anchorage among Picts,
where he might, with his twelve, declare the Faith
against the Druids. So Conal let us go,
provisioned well: we sailed northwest by north,
near Islay coasting close, past Jura's Paps,
Colonsay, Oronsay, until we struck
the studded islands to the south of Mull;
and there, on the vigil eve of Pentecost,
we sighted Iona, and every heart aboard,
with a great leaping, knew we'd found our haven.
And ere we grounded in a rocky creek
our master rose in the bow and blest the land,
bidding Druids and their demons flee,
and we rowed in and safely disembarked.

AXALL: And other voices we have heard before,
Conan's who shared with him by Foyle's green shore
the last sad watch, and those who knew his days
in Derry's shelter, rich with love and praise,
shall tell, as each has proved by sweat and grace,
the founding of another holy place.

MONK A: We raised our first huts, they were more like
windbreaks,
in those hard days, above the eastern shore
where Alban currachs could float timber in,
and later the full cargoes we had trysted;
and when we all were housed with stock and store,
we squared the rough stones for the Mother Church
and started building.

MONK B: And a few of us,
trained to the craft, flung and dragged in the seine,
for fish are fish whatever seas they swim,
and the same labour needed for the catch.

MONK C: We also cleared and ploughed the shallow earth,
and let frost split the scraws that first hard winter,
and sowed our oats in spring, and after reaping,
threshed the small sheaves and drew them chanting down

in slipes of our devising, every task
an act of prayer, all men one family.
MONK A: There was a bog above the ring of huts
with little tufted lochs, where waterfowl
jerked through the sighing rushes; from the lochs
a narrow burn ran down into the creek
with force enough to turn the wooden wheel
and grind our corn. We built a little kiln
to dry the oats reaped between Lammas showers.
We had our smithy where familiar skills
wrought gridiron, kettle, pan and pot and ploughshare
and cranes and hooks and chains to swing our pots.
MONK B: And on the rocky places we bred up
our blackfaced hardy flock, and herded kine,
for wool to spin and weave, for hides and butter.
CONAN: All this labour under Columcille's eye
and with his blessing, so full charged with grace,
that I have heard our brethren in the fields
tell how, around them, stocking the reaped oats,
ricking the hay, or piling stone upon stone
to fence the pasture, suddenly there'd come
a whiff of perfume like the beans in blossom,
the airs of Paradise come down on earth.
AXALL: The island shed its perfume to the world,
and as a wandering bee will seek the furled
throat of the blossom for its nurturing,
then, nectar laden, open happy wing
and hurry with report to its own kind;
for north and east and south, by every wind
the curraghs came with men in search of grace,
hunted and outcast some, as from the chase
wounded or weary; some with kingly state
their galleys with gilt planking 'maculate,
offering tribute and demanding peace,
which till they grounded their pride stiffened knees,
the Abbot Columcille was loath to give;
nay, swifter blessed the moaning fugitive
than the proud noble, shewd more open hand
to landless peasant than to lord of land.

Yet this good service seemed but half his task,
for while he laboured, Alba seemed to ask
his voice among the tribes by firth and glen,
feud-urgent princes, foray-driving men.
So when he saw that he might safely leave
the island-brotherhood to grow and thrive
without his presence, he set forth once more
this time to Alba with its fretted shore.

CONAN: Our purpose was to face the Pictish King,
Brude, who in northern fastness held his court,
that we might win him to the Grace of God.
So we went out, the Abbot and a band
of tried retainers, Comgall, Canice and I;
first by the waters along the narrow lochs,
then over mountain passes, through thick forest,
dragging in bog and wading roaring burns,
bedding in heather or with lonely herds,
when chance threw up a wisp of smoke among
the crowded pinetops or between the hills
where the scored rock divides the flooded moss.

DEMAL: It was a land to break the bravest heart,
trackless and barren, where each cleft would start
its spitting wildcat, where wolves tracked the deer
and tore the tall stag down in mad career,
where badgers roamed at dusk and yelping fox
left its hot stench upon the splintered rocks,
where stones would fall and bound, till, out of sight,
you'd hear them drop in pot-holes deep as night;
and the white torrents tumbled down to dash
over the black scree with a sleety splash;
and cruising eagle near the pallid sun
sought for storm-wildered hind to batter on;
and the awed silence of the snowy peak
bid the heart fear the avalanche should break,
then the withdrawing steps on creaking ice
along the toothed edge of the precipice.

CONAN: Then from the rubbled shore of a long loch
we saw the castle clawed upon a ledge
like some fierce brooding monster. Every man

stopped his step dismayed. It seemed beyond
the reach of our tired bodies and spent wits.
The washed air shewed each coign, but we could guess
a hard league gapped the bowl of space between.
Then Comgall spoke at last.

COMGALL: O Columcille,
can we endure this yet? Must we go on,
with each slow step subtracting from our hope?

CONAN: But Columcille stood as in reverie,
not heeding us. Then Canice loud complained—

CANICE: This is a devil's country. Every tree
and rock is charged with evil against us,
and there in the heart of evil its master sits,
plotting his terrors, ordering his demons
to turn the stone beneath our bleeding feet,
to stab the breath with unexpected hillocks,
or fling a fist of hailstones in the face.

COMGALL: Yet safe in Iona you made a prophecy
that we should conquer after many trials.
Columcille, does your prophecy still hold?

COLUMCILLE: My prophecies are always logical,
not hinged on wonder or coincidence,
but as men say what change of wind brings rain
from years of weather in the laboured fields.
I may not know each leap my logic takes
more than the joiner gazing on the plank
and seeing well what shafts he'll trim from it.
The King will see us, and although his Druids
will strive against us with their apes and imps—
mere stinging flies to such as fought the gales—
he'll treat us fairly, even be baptised—

CANICE: For you will humble him with miracles
and whip him into submission, all his clan?

COLUMCILLE: Not so, Canice. It will be policy
that makes his strong knee bend. He is alone,
a petty king between two mounting powers.
The Dalriadans press him; and around
his outer isles the Norse marauders slip
to rape and pillage the small villages.

Brude will think better as a Christian king
allied by faith to countless royal cousins
whose banners star the tents of Christendom,
joined in a common and united front,
than stand outside and fall a prey to both
the warring Christians—and the warring Norse.

CANICE: This sounds not like the former Columcille,
who never stopped to watch a game or battle,
but tucked his long skirts up and joined the fray,
trumpeting victory for his chosen side.

COLUMCILLE: There you are just, Canice; but pray remember,
the blessed island years have altered me.
Withdrawn by edict from my Ulster home,
I've learnt withdrawal in my lonely heart.
This sick world needs the blustering busy man
eager in action. But far more it needs
the man of thought and prayer and meditation,
for when the busy man's thronged day's accomplished,
there's still the judgement and the last Assize,
and only prayer can school the wilful heart
in disciplines which prosper out of time ...
But we are rested. Let the next steep league
be the last round of some Olympic game.
Forward together, chanting as we go.

CONAN: We kept in step so long as ground allowed it,
then fell in single file after Columcille;
heartened, 'tis true, but still the weariness
of all the times and leagues of travelling,
tugged at our muscles, hung about our thoughts,
and now and then we stumbled to our knees,
or panted on a rock, or stooped to cup
the bogbrown water in our brier-torn hands.
But sudden, looking up from our distress,
we saw the castle like a burnished cliff
astride the rough track we had chanced upon.
We could but march ahead to the very door.
Already watchers in the topmost turrets
shook weapons at us and as quick withdrew.
And as we paused to still our fluttering pulses

on the smooth grassy sward before the castle,
we saw at once the great doors firmly shut,
and no man came to ask the password of us.
We seemed to front and face the final cliff
that shewed no foothold for the venturemost,
and yet Iona was worlds away.
This was an end of something. Comgall spoke.

COMGALL: O Abbot Columcille;
King Brude provides no welcome for us here;
and we are weary, weary, travelspent.
Must we then squat and hunker by these walls
while there is meat and drink and warmth beyond?

COLUMCILLE: Call once then, Comgall. That their charity
may hear and echo to the last Assize.
[COMGALL *calls.*]

COMGALL: No answer, Master, only my own voice
shrunk to a breathless echo; and the pigeons
flapping and flustering farther up the cliff.

CANICE: Are these not a good omen, Columcille?
Where pigeons find a footing we should find
a nest and crevice for the Holy Spirit,
a tufted sod of thrift and heathy flowers.

COLUMCILLE: My Comgall, we have come a tedious way.
Shod with our purpose we have journeyed so
that rock and water could not hinder us.
Are we defeated then by planks and hinges?
Is this blank door to be our coffin lid?
Come closer brothers; we shall enter now.
See, I but make the blessed Sign of the Cross,
and push it gently with my open hand.
[*Sound of grating door*]

COMGALL: Forgive me, Master, forgive my lack of faith.
My heart was marvel-brimmed and could not hold
another drop of wonder.

CONAN: You shall see far greater marvels yet.

COLUMCILLE: Why stand we here? Approach and follow me.

CONAN: The doors lay wide now, open to the world,
and we were on the threshold of the castle,
a long roofed hall before us thronged with men.

We paused and gaped, but Columcille advanced.
We stumbled after, silently, our hearts
loud in our ears. The men were arm'd men,
clutching their spears, or holding ready blades:
and as we moved upon them they drew back,
dividing as the waters of the sea
when Moses led the Israelites across;
but silently, save for the shuffled feet
and the quick breathing of the shouldered mob.
Then some let fall their swords, and some dropped down,
clashing their greaves upon the paven floor.
Slowly we ventured in the Abbot's wake,
each step—a step into eternity;
half-dreading that we'd hear the great doors clang
behind us like a trap. But Columcille
strode gravely on, until, along the lane
of breathing soldiers, we could see ahead
a tall man with a high and antlered helmet
step from a dais—and an empty chair,
and move with equal pace toward Columcille.
Behind him, in the shelter of his cloak,
were some crouched figures in the Druid's garb,
mouthing, grimacing, fingering the air,
and pointing at us with their crooked nails.
I lived far longer in that castle hall,
pacing its twenty or its thirty yards,
than all the years before or after that.
Then at time's end they met, six feet between,
the tall armed King, the tall and comely Abbot;
each stood and looked to each, with no word said.
Then when the minutes beat like torture drops,
slowly the King spoke with a quiet voice.

KING: What men are these that doors swing open to,
that brush the oaken slats aside like threads?
Who is your master? What's your errand here?

COLUMCILLE: We come from Heaven's King to bring relief
to any heart oppressed by the world's weight.
We offer mercy like an open door.

KING: For any heart oppressed by the world's weight?

Then I have tarried long for your approach,
for I am weary of my warring days,
tossed like a twig upon conflicting tides.
What is the password to your place of Peace?
COLUMCILLE: You must kneel humbly, bowing your proud head,
and say 'I wait, Lord; come into my heart,
inhabit all my members, make me Thine.'
HIGH KING: This is too simple. Let there be a spell,
a muttering of spells and coiling smokes,
and a harsh trial—and a sacrifice.
COLUMCILLE: The trial's still to come. The sacrifice
is made already, for the Son of God
offered Himself for you, and was accepted.
We have no spells to stuff the ears with noise.
We whisper reason to the open mind,
and sing salvation to the open heart.
Kneel, in the Name of Father, Son and Spirit.
KING: I feel an anguish beating in my breast.
My blood turns water and my sinews fail.
VOICES: He kneels. He kneels.
DRUID: King Brude, remember Dagon and your fathers.
This is a necromancer pounding you
in his cold mortar. Fight against his will.
COLUMCILLE: Not my will, Brude. The cunning will of God
that crams the forest in a single seed,
and out of imperfection draws perfection,
thumbing the stuff of Chaos into Shape,
and weaving your tossed twig into a hurdle
to fold his flock in safety. Say: 'I wait,
Lord; come into my heart; inhabit all
my members; make me Thine'.
KING: I wait—I wait—Lord, come into my heart.
CONAN: O there was singing in the Courts of Heaven;
I heard it as you hear the winter stars
bright in the frost sing star to lonely star,
linked to the chorus of the constellations.
And as a counter bass the Druid's rage,
loud for dethroning, loud for banishment.
huddled in corners, strewing bitter herbs,

and chanting consternation to their foe.
Then, one by one, the King's men paid their homage
not to an earthly king but to the Lord,
and were baptized and blessed and rose free men.

AXALL: This was a moment I had waited for;
the man I guarded now was something more
than one bright soul to cherish; by his power
and virtue, he contained a multitude,
rallied to mercy, won to brotherhood;
and if I could prevent his falling off,
he'd add a nation to the hosts above.
Now I had risen from a single fight
to captaincy among the crowds of light;
and Demal whining could but creep away
droning his 'Nay' against my trumpet 'Yea'.

DEMAL: I play for time. I've seen conversion come
in royal progress, loud with fife and drum,
and like black ants, the little brittle souls
march in the sunlight from their secret holes
for one bright moment, till a skift of rain
shall send them pelting for their holes again.
It's not what sweeps through masses that I fear,
for, by their nature, I can shortly steer
their drive in what direction I may please.
It's one man in his cell upon his knees
who bests my challenge longest. I can break
a faggot easier than a single stick.

CONAN: So though the King desired our sojourn with him,
when all was measured, leaving Canice there
to teach the learners, Columcille withdrew
in the King's galley round the broken coast,
to harbour with us safe again at Iona.
[*Seafaring theme throughout this speech as background*]
Then settled once again among his people
his only family now, the island few,
the Abbot laboured in his place with prayer,
devising order to contain our days,
filling the hours with miracles of sense,
weaving our threads into a single garment

spreading a cloak of comfort in the waste,
till Iona became the Banner of Christendom,
and Columcille was master of the Kings
all over Alba, setting this one up
and that one casting down. His influence
was the sole charter any prince desired
who wished to prosper to the seat of state.
But out of all their embassies and homage
one moment stood flame-cinctured, charged with danger,
the crowning of the King when Conal died;
for his succession was a tangled skein,
knotted with flaws and barbed with secret thorns.

DEMAL: O I had spun a web that would entice
and tangle fast that buzzing Lord of Flies,
for Columcille, so vast his eager pride,
must plunge and thresh till every limb was tied
in the sheer muddle of conflicting claims,
of usages, of families, of names.
I put you to the test, my Angel friend,
for, till this instant, you and I but lend
mere hands and wills to shaping circumstance,
but now you too are hauled into the dance,
no more ringside patron with advice
when the steps falter and the tired blows miss.

AXALL: Never before had I to part the screen,
step on the stage, and crudely intervene
and front my truant ward thus face to face.

CONAN: Garvan had followed Conal, but his death
at Pictish hands, had swept him off the board.
Of his two sons, the elder, Aidan, had
the clearer right, but Columcille preferred
the younger, Eoghan, as his closer friend,
and would not send to crown the elder brother.
So then in Dalriada the contest rose,
some for Prince Aidan, some for Columcille's choice,
and troubled by approaching civil war,
the country lay an open prey to any
marauding reiver from the barren hills
or mountainy chieftain with a score of spears.

AXALL: I stood one night within the Abbot's cell,
    bid from above, in urgency to tell
    rash Columcille his stubborn wilfulnesss
    ran counter in his choice to the decrees
    of Heaven, which ordained the elder crowned
    as firmer rooted in the common ground
    than his frail brother, though the Abbot's heart
    inclined to him who drew the lesser part
    of the affections of the crownless folk:
    this clearly written in a crystal book
    I carried with me. But the Abbot lay
    on his hard boards, in sleep a castaway,
    far from my signal; and he would not wake
    though light was round him like a new daybreak.
DEMAL: But Columcille let that night pass, and when
    day spread and faded, and he came again
    to sleep, he came without a memory of
    the visitation from the Place Above.
AXALL: I came the second night, my book in hand,
    but he nor waked nor heeded its command;
    and on the third night I returned again,
    armed by my orders, not to stand in vain
    before the sleeper, but to shock his reason
    into a sober state of penitence,
    in which, convicted of his stubborn treason,
    he'd find relief in swift obedience.
DEMAL: But I had schooled that treason long and well:
    that instant he rocked slowly on the brink of Hell.
AXALL: I cross the cell and touch him. He will rise,
    the baffled wonder blinking in his eyes.
COLUMCILLE: What is it, Axall? If it still is you
    in this harsh armoured guise? Or but a trick
    of my own enemy who always waits
    to trip my faltering step—and bring me down.
AXALL: You know me well. You know my errand here:
    I come once more as Heaven's messenger
    to bid you give your suffrage and the crown,
    not to your friend, but to the elder son.
COLUMCILLE: The crown to Aidan! I have raised my hand

for Eoghan, and none other wins my voice.

AXALL: You have your little reasons; they must bow.
It is the voice of Heaven commands you now!

COLUMCILLE: So has the tempter tried me many a time;
but I'll not yield. I am no doting bishop
nudged to assent by a conspiring priest
hot from dark cabal he's reeking with.

AXALL: Heaven's temper rises, stubborn Columcille!
Would you inch further, draw the terrible
Anger of God upon your errant soul?
I've sought by grace to guard you, safe and whole,
from Hell's cold plotting, from your own mad pride
that roared through Ireland, frantic patricide;
and by that grace redeemed, your voice in prayer
has drawn down comfort from the shining air,
and shed a blessing on the troubled land;
and by that grace your never-weary hand
has wrought its mercies, with a saintly art,
on the scarred tablets of a sinner's heart.
Will you not heed me? I who am your friend,
who still will see your play out to the end
with anxious love. Why must you strive with me
like some vext child that wrestles to be free
from the firm hand and the protective arm
that safe would shield him from the waiting harm?

COLUMCILLE: So lisps the tempter with seductive phrase,
mining below my strong-built resolution
with wheedling memories of my other self
before I was anointed of the Lord
to bear his pennant through the hosting kings.

AXALL: O that sick pride again! Your fever mounts
to brace you to the last of your affronts.
Now and forever answer or I strike.
Do you obey the book?

COLUMCILLE: I do not.

AXALL: This is Heaven's Anger like a thunder stroke
that by your wilful blindness you provoke.
[*He strikes* COLUMCILLE. *Crack of a whip. Sound of* COLUMCILLE *falling.*]

COLUMCILLE: O Lord forgive me. Come into this heart,
　　shattered with pride, and make me wholly Thine.
　　Inhabit tall my members: make me Thine;
　　and what Thy will is I shall haste to do.
AXALL: The mercy I have known I share with you.
　　Rise up forgiven. Yet for Mercy's sake,
　　and lest again the gale of pride should break,
　　forever shall this weal upon your side
　　recall the toppling crisis of your pride.
　　[*Music of a rather wailing kind continued throughout next speech, but fading*]
CONAN: And in the morning when I sought the Abbot,
　　he moaned and wept upon his narrow bed
　　and bade me send for Aidan to be King,
　　and bared me the sore bruise along his side
　　that he wore ever after. [*Fade*]
DEMAL: I'd find it hard to say which one of us
　　emerged from that last bout victorious
　　but though who's victor's difficult to name,
　　it's clear the Abbot cannot lodge his claim.
　　I might well leave him stricken, sure to fall,
　　and seek new duties at my Master's call.
　　An emperor in high Byzantium
　　already riots gaily to his doom,
　　and could I choose I should be there to see.
　　And there's a rabid prince in Tartary
　　that hacks his steps out bluntly with a sword
　　and climbs to kingship of the Mongol horde—
　　a noble spectacle; and Ctesiphon
　　drifts deep in sand, one thrust and it has gone.
AXALL: So near defeated that you would withdraw?
　　Have you forgotten it is Heaven's law
　　which keeps us locked in combat till the end;
　　our place and purpose still is here my friend.
　　Yet I have struck him, and his noble flesh
　　must wear the wound upon it, raw and fresh,
　　and I am injured too, in that my rage
　　dragged me unthinking out upon the stage,
　　among the shapes of coarse mortality

whose influence and power should only be
a whisper or a sudden flash of light,
a dream, a mood, a portent in the night
a falling star, a drifting thread in air,
the heart's own answer to the heart's own prayer.
We may not rest but we may slacken grip:
leave Columcille like to a battered ship,
now the storm's over, safely still to ride
on the swift waters of the running tide.

CONAN: And in the days that followed, the Abbot's heart
was set austerely to chastise the flesh.
He laid such penance on himself we feared
that he might die and leave us fatherless.

MONK A: I cannot say if this be true or not:
my memory does not aid me in this matter
of what the sand was like upon the shore
after the tide ran out. But I have seen
our Abbot lie and moan upon the beach
and cry for mercy; and some say it was
his sharp starved ribs imprinted in the sand
that are remembered by the ripple marks,
a sign forever of his lonely strife
and promise of our peace.

DERMAID: There was a day
he met a ragged hag along the waste,
and as his custom was he spoke to her.

COLUMCILLE: What seek you here, good mother, in the waste?
There are no berries yet, of tufted wool
to pluck from off the thorns and save to spin.

HAG: O Holy Father I seek nettles here.

COLUMCILLE: Nettles? The stinging kind for chastisement
of the rebellious flesh? But you are old,
and there is little lust can vex you now.

HAG: My penance is my poverty, Holy Father.
I gather nettles for my daily broth,
for in this season there is nothing else for me to eat.

COLUMCILLE: Then there is poverty
surpassing mine in its simplicity.
My thanks, good mother, you have taught me much.

While anyone walks hungry through the world
I have no charter to indulge myself:
I'll dine off nettles too. But Dermaid, see
that this old mother has a bag of meal
and a full pail of milk. I stand condemned
in that my charity has withered up
in the dry air of thought and meditation
too long enjoyed.

DERMAID: So he insisted strong;
and nettles were his fare in the bare season.
and though we tried, preparing them, to fat
their leanness up with butter and with cream
and secret fists of meal, he never failed
to smell the luxury and spit it out
and whip us with his tongue for our deceit.

MONK A: O he was tender to the least of things.
A heron came from Ireland, from the west,
weary and heavy in its dragging flight,
and fell before him and he had her fed
with salted fish and cherished her three days
till she grew strong and stalked behind his stride
like a wise deacon, when he left his cell
to watch us labour. Then, one evening
our Abbot said that we must meet at dawn
to bid her kindly faring on her way.
And the grey heron made a throaty noise,
and Columcille commanded us to hear
that she took leave of us, and knew her grief
at parting from such friends, but stronger yet
the ties that bound her to her native lochs,
and she must go again into the west,
as he would go if but the Will of God
could lift the exile-sentence from his heart.

CONAN: In these years now King Aidan grew his friend
from Dalriada oft would journey over
for his good fellowship and steady counsel.
But once he came deep troubled in his mind,
for the High King of Ireland had demanded,
since Aidan's fathers once had come from Antrim,

that tribute should be paid, and homage done,
as from a subordinate-prince to his overlord,
and ordered Aidan to appear before him
where Hugh, the High King, gathered at Drumceat
his underlords for homage, and gave law
to all his kingdom, brought together there.

AIDAN: And not mere tribute but the threat of war
if I withold it. Shall a king endure,
because he is a little king, the sword
close to his throat so pointed, that he make
a shameful peace of bondage, or bring down
terror upon his people and defeat.
If there is justice in the halls of kings
speak for me, Columcille, that I be heard.
And yet at his stern conclave the High King
holds at Drumceat, not merely my fate alone,
but other issues wait upon your counsel.
But, chief of all, the Irish poets are threatened
by the uneasy lords who grudge their keep
and would expel them from the Irish Kingdom.
Come then with me: the High King, at Drumceat,
will offer royal judgment after debate
with the wisest conclave ever met in Ulster.
Dare you, the greatest Ulsterman, be absent?

COLUMCILLE: You know I cannot go. The sentence that binds me
forbids my eyes to look on Irish ground.
And yet, and yet, the poets have my suffrage,
and Aidan, you are dear to me as breath.

AIDAN: You must come. The nation's judgment needs you.
Is there no way?—The sentence you have borne
has been wiped out by service. None would rebuke you
if you went back. The glory of Iona
would shut the mouths that once had dared to accuse.

COLUMCILLE: I wore my penance humbly. Shall I now
fling it aside because my selfish temper
sees chance to use my power in the old proud way?

AIDAN: Forbids you look on Ireland? Must you look?
There surely is some way to meet this challenge.
The sentence was to curb you, not to keep

your powerul voice from service to your nation.
Surely some way? There is. Now listen, Columcille.
Could not a cloth bound closely round your eyes
fulfil the letter? And you would not see,
and still would have good eyes for fair Iona.

COLUMCILLE: I do not like it Aidan. It is a trick.
Yet if I do not see ...? I still could perform
with prayer and counsel that which I realise
is a solemn duty it were wrong to avoid.

AIDAN: Not a trick, my Master, rather say a device
to gain the greater good. You could don the bandage
just before sight of Ireland and wear it close
till blessed Iona peeps over the waves again.

COLUMCILLE: For the threatened poets, Aidan, and for you.
make the ships ready. I shall go with you.

AXALL: Our seeming-truce was but the interval
when wrestlers pause to muster breath—and call
up the tired limbs' reserves, for the last throw.
The galleys leave for Eire; we must go.
[*Seafaring theme and fade out*]

DEMAL: I am before you. I have set the snare.
The High King's tent stands in an open square
among the lesser Lodges; and within,
the wife of Hugh, the dark relentless Queen,
plans with her counsellor to bind and knot
tomorrow's trial in a perfect plot
to beat the poets whose satiric rimes
with whips of wit had stripped her many times.

COUNSELLOR: Good Queen, I am impatient for tomorrow.
Do you think I have left too much to chance?

QUEEN: You worked well, Counsellor, I hardly needed
to add my voice to weight the High King's resolution
to rid this island of the troublesome poets,
and assert his privilege over Aidan.
You had the High King well schooled in the arguments.
[*A knock without*]

COUNSELLOR: There's someone outside, my Lady, shall I go
to learn his errand?

QUEEN: Go; see who it is.

COUNSELLOR: It's the King of Leinster, Crimen Kean, who waits:
    he carries news that's urgent for your Lord.
QUEEN: We cannot wake him. Bid Crimen Kean come in.
CRIMEN: Your Majesty. The High King must learn my news.
QUEEN: He cannot come. I'll bear it to him myself.
COUNSELLOR: What's pressing so my Lord?
CRIMEN: Fantastic news: that Columcille returns.
QUEEN: Columcille! He's forbidden to set foot
    on Irish ground.
CRIMEN: Forbidden, yes; but not to come: to see.
COUNSELLOR: Aye. That's the penance
    old Molaish laid on him these thirty years.
QUEEN: But how to come without the act of sight?
CRIMEN: Comes blindfold, Lady, that he may not see,
    but comes that he may speak.
QUEEN: Who told you this?
CRIMEN: The ships already have come up the Foyle,
    and now they camp at Roe-mouth, to resume
    their morning voyage here.
COUNSELLOR: King Aidan's ships!
    We might have guessed he'd summon every aid
    to help him in his disobedience.
QUEEN: But Columcille too is a poet, he comes to defend them.
    And are they not my savagest enemies?
COUNSELLOR: Aye, Lady: they have made their cleverest verses
    strike at your royal person. But Columcille—
CRIMEN: You must not fear so, Lady.
    As I learn his task is Aidan's debt,
    to try to avert it; it is a petty cause.
QUEEN: But Columcille is headstrong.
COUNSELLOR: He was; his age must tell
    against his leaping temper.
QUEEN: Old men are worse, peevish, dogmatic, crazed,
    not easily to be thwarted, stiff with opinion,
    looking for insults, touchy and quarrelsome.
COUNSELLOR: Your Lord, my master, has never been his foe.
    Columcille's obedient now and quiet paced;
    so overlaid with saintliness, he nods.
    I do not fear what he'll say, but rather his name ...

CRIMEN: Yes. That's the danger; out of sympathy
    even the King might incline to him.
QUEEN: Not Hugh, good Leinster. He remembers the fate
    that followed the copied parchment. He will not heed him.
    Still, we must be on our guard; not rouse or provoke
    old Columcille, but courteously with smiling,
    keeping him well bemused with gentle words.
CRIMEN: My own dread is that when I have spoken
    against the poets, he will be moved to reply.
COUNSELLOR: He will be too old and tired to bother with that.
    It's only a personal loyalty to his friend
    will open his toothless mouth.
    [*Fade-up noise of assembled crowd*]
HERALD: Silence for Crimen Kean, the King of Leinster!
CRIMEN: My Lord and King, the three provincial Kings
    have bid me state our case against the poets,
    and not kings only, every subordinate prince
    joins with us in the challenge.
    These useless poets swarming over the land
    are locusts that eat our substance up. They come
    with their fat teams, like tinkers in a clan,
    revelling, drunken, marching thro' the land,
    demanding shelter, ending with possession:
    First, a seat by the fire and a sup of broth,
    then, by degrees, half of the host's own bed.
    If a man be strong
    and holds to his own right they hurl their rimes
    at his poor head, until the children cry
    over the walls at him, or at his people.
    His servants leave him; none will work for him.
    [*Crowd cry assent*]
    My Lord, High King, you know their arrogance.
    Have they not bid you give them up the brooch
    no King dare part with? Without deference
    they stood before you, taunting even you
    with stanza-thrust.
VOICES: It's true enough—the rascals.
CRIMEN: It's a hundred years
    since, as old men will bear witness, poets worked

in field or quarry. They are fat and slow,
with jewelled fingers, paunchy in their robes,
while we must plow and sow and mow and thrash
and stagger with the full sack at their bidding
to bake their bread. They neither spin nor weave,
yet wear apparel we cannot afford.
[*Voices assenting*]
If a man here in Erinn, has a son
whose face is dirty out of laziness,
whose hands are smooth because he will not work
these poets call to him as they pass,
offer him wealth and plenty for a mere trick
accomplished sitting with a pen in hand,
and find him a kindly prince to batten on
till he has eaten him to beggary,
and then goes off to find a richer victim;
for they grow more rapacious with their years
till they are monstrous like Dallan Forgael here.
[*Voices jeering and laughing*]

DALLAN FORGAEL: High King, protection. I am old and blind,
grown old with service to your royal person.

VOICES: Service? Hear his insolence.

HIGH KING: Peace, Dallan Forgael; he but states his case.
It shall not go unbalanced.

VOICES: He spoke the truth. There is no answer to it.

DALLAN: Crimen Kean,
you fraction princeling, I shall make a rime
will bring the blisters to your foolish face—

CRIMEN: O hear this braggart—

DALLAN: And leave your name a synomym for dirt,
if you provoke me further. [*Uproar of crowd*]

HIGH KING: Forgael, peace. [*Uproar diminishes*]
Leinster, continue, I forbid his threats.
[*Background still of murmurs quieting to—*]

CRIMEN: My Lord; two fates can only come of this.
The nation sinks distracted, impoverished,
while these gross maggots perish with the flesh
they aptly poisoned, and desolation rules:
[*Crowd agrees*]

or we expel the poets, make them men forbid,
and set them on Britain to devour that land.
VOICES: Expel them! Expel them! Drive them out.
CRIMEN: My voice with those who here companion me
is for their abolition from this day.
Make it a crime against the King and State
for any man to drive the trade of verse.
And if a poet be taken
strolling the roads, or sitting by a hearth,
with rimes upon his lips, or wearing the habit
of the six bright colours,
let him be stripped and whipped and sold a slave.
[*Crowd assents, with a voice or two of protest*]
My Lord,
our fathers let this cancerous breed increase,
seeing no danger in one crazy poet
who, without rime, has still got charity.
We must not let one poet remain in Erinn
or he will breed his kind by swift contagion.
The slogan's 'Root and Branch'; destroy or expel.
[*Crowd applauds*]
VOICES: Expel the poets. This is the end of the poets!
HIGH KING: My Lord and Counsellors. The charge is laid.
Shall I call on Dallan Forgael to reply
as the Chief Poet?
VOICES: No, not Dallan Forgael—He will insult us.
Ask Columcille. Ask Columcille to speak.
HERALD: Silence, my Lords, the High King lifts his hand.
[*Further but reduced babble*]
Silence I pray you Sirs, the High King speaks.
HIGH KING: Will you speak, Columcille, or are you weary
with all this bickering and shrill debate?
COLUMCILLE: I will speak, Hugh, for the poet,
if none else speak.
HIGH KING: Then first I warn you. There are witnesses
for every phrase that seemed extravagant
in Crimen Kean's indictment.
[*Voices of assent*]
HERALD: Sirs, Columcille the Abbot of Iona

would have your patience.

COLUMCILLE: High King and Kings and Counsellors, this day
you have heard so many words you must be tired;
and now you must listen a while to an old man
garrulous with his years. Yet courteously
you will keep silent and appear to hear him,
because the things he wishes to declare
are greater than any weakness in his manner.
   [*Crowd murmurs doubtfully*]

VOICE: Go on, Columcille. There's nothing you can say.

DALLAN: Speak for the menaced poets Columcille.
   [*Crowd cry against* DALLAN FORGAEL]

COLUMCILLE: As Crimen Kean has said: these banded poets
have laid a tax upon your economy
hard to be borne.There have been drunken poets,
revellers, bawdy rimers and satirists
who hurt the hand that feeds them recklessly.
   [*Voices assent here and there*]
Fire is an inconstant element;
it burns the proud house down, it scorches the fingers,
it licks and runs and ruins till it's quenched.
Sometimes too great to quench, it must be left
to ebb and die in its own bitter ash.
Yet fire's a fellow labourer, if held
in a hard vessel and replenished well:
it roasts the meat: it boils a pot of water:
it bakes the bread, it dries the traveller's cloak;
it bends the rigid iron to the shapes
we have for metal.

VOICES: What's all this to do with the poets?

COLUMCILLE: In a crusie lamp fire lights the whole house up;
it warns the ship
to steer outside the craggy cape. It warms
the thin fingers of the aged man.

CRIMEN: But we are not old men. Our hands are hot.

COLUMCILLE: The stuff the poets play with is a fire,
and, like a fire, has uses manifold.
I must not weary you with counting them.

CRIMEN: Thanks good Abbot, we ourselves can count.

[*Voices assenting*]

VOICE: Let the Abbot speak.

COLUMCILLE: Let these suffice for the uses of poetry.
    It warms the chill heart with a snatch of song.
    It shines a steady witness to the truth.
    It gives a flame to men when duty's slack
    and cannot move them. And it scorches vice
    with its live tongues till the heart is clean as a bone.

DALLAN: You hear. You cravens hear the blessed truth.
    [*Dissenting voices*]

COLUMCILLE: But there is more. The blessed thing is freedom;
    freedom to choose to go or not to go,
    freedom to choose—this is the knife edge here.
    For freedom to be gentle implies the freedom
    also to be cruel, and, therefore, stakes
    a soul's fate on a single right of choice.
    Poets are men, and should as men be free.
    I cannot give my voice to one who urges
    that men be free to fight, and yet not free to rime:

VOICE: That's fair enough.

COLUMCILLE: And further upon this, the written word
    was written to be read. All scholarship
    is as a reliquary of the past,
    and half our knowledge is cut in the stone of verse.
    Cuchullain and Ulysses and the singing David—
    Is there, because a handful here and there
    are wilful men,
    to be no more remembrance of these names,
    nor new names added to the tally of rime?

VOICES: No. No.

COLUMCILLE: Then should this Kingdom shuffle into the dark
    among unstoried people, to be forgotten,
    and Crimen Kean be never heard of more
    for all his acts of daring?
    [*Some laughter in crowd— cries of 'Good for you' and 'Poor Crimen
    Kean'*]
    So I say,
    for freedom's sake and for the worth of the craft,
    let poets live and prosper under rule,

that you, High King with reasoned counselling,
set up by statute limiting their power,
their rights and numbers, clearly laying down,
by rule and definition how they shall live.
I crave your pardon for my tediousness.
[*Great ovation*]

*The following page is missing in the manuscript. The debate
continues.*

for benefits received from his support
he chid them from him, bid them offer court
to one more worthy. He would have no praise
while yet he lived on Earth. In after days
he would have joy enough in what was done,
till then they'd give their praise to Mary's Son.
CONAN: But Master Abbot, surely you will take
one song of praise from Dallan Forgael here;
he is the High Bard of the riming craft,
and fitter than a flock of little songs
were one deep eagle-anthem from his heart.
COLUMCILLE: Not even he must praise me while I live.
DALLAN: But Abbot, this is wrong. I have the right
to praise your name that any poet has.
Our bardic rules are firm. I make my verse,
and you must pay me for my making it.
COLUMCILLE: If after I am dead your wish persists
then rime away and give me of your best.
DALLAN: Yet make your payment now. I'd rather know
what you would give me now than after death.
COLUMCILLE: You shall have kine and horses, silver and gold.
DALLAN: No such reward shall I accept from you,
for these I may expect from any king
and better quality than you'd provide.
COLUMCILLE: I'll give you the Kingdom to go in.
DALLAN: I may not take it. I must earn that right,
by my own life and work deserving it.
COLUMCILLE: I'll bear a soul to Heaven on your behalf
for every thread you number in your cloak.

DALLAN: I will not take it; for what virtue lies
  in this poor garment shouldered round my age?
COLUMCILLE: I'll found a little church and name it yours
  and heaven to all that shall be buried there.
DALLAN: I am no tonsured fellow to pace out
  the saint's old discipline. I am a man
  and may, before I die, fall into ways
  that would not muster blessing round my name.
COLUMCILLE: O Dallan Forgael, you have bargained hard;
  your better craft were in the marketplace.
  This I shall bid against you holding out
  my open hand for yours to strike agreed,
  that anyone whose memory'll grip your poem
  and can repeat it word by golden word
  shall win to Heaven for the sake of it.
DALLAN: This payment I shall take and thank you for it.
CONAN: This is a strange reward in such a case.
  Shall anyone, a lecher or a fool,
  remembering the stanzas in their order,
  avoid the proper penance for his deeds
  and wrap his sins up in this single poem?
  This is near heresy. Have you the power—?
COLUMCILLE: I have no power. The poetry's the power;
  the nature of the words determines it.
  Have you known any kind, mean, hypocrite,
  lecher, or fool, liar, cruel, knave,
  who could repeat a noble poem through
  with not one faltering syllable? Their lies,
  cruelties, follies and hypocrisies
  shutter their hearts against it. They must fail.
  This is a simple test of quality,
  for goodness speaks to goodness evermore.
  [*Seafaring theme and fade*]
CONAN: Returning to Iona, worn with travel,
  he found the pagan tide had risen up
  and threatened his low walls. With summoned strength,
  he thrust the dark clouds back, and light resumed
  its rocky sconce and brought day back again
  over the Alban highlands, lochs and firths,

till all was peace again and his wise rule
lay like an Autumn on the mellow world.
But constellations move, and seasons turn,
and the bright frost of winter touched his heart
with the sharp warning that he soon must leave
his old bones cold within the mounded earth,
and send his soul on strange new wanderings,
far from Iona and the brotherhood.

DEMAL: I'd left him so and gone on other tasks
assuming various attitudes and masks
in other dramas, had my due success
in once-kind hearts ground into bitterness,
in rash men wrecked by folly, and betrayed
by the ironic humours of my trade.
For I have dreamed that Columcille, grown old
and weak with age, should find his flesh too cold
for the hot heart within him, and descend,
split by the tumult, to a foolish end.

AXALL: But as his mortal dress grew frail and thin,
the great heart's glory stronger shone within,
and the high soul in saintly loveliness
moved like a glowing aureole to bless
the salted air it stirred, the stony ground
that soon must close the mortal body's wound.
And when at last, as his death hour had come,
safe in Iona, blessed island home,
and yet not home, for all were exile there,
the faithful Dermaid, who had lead with care
his failing steps out to the harvest field,
now led him gently back that he might yield
the last breath up where he had known so well
the pit and peak of Mercy, his stone cell,
and laid him there to rest the last hour out.
A young monk came to phrase some private doubt
and know it answered, unaware the end
winged close about his Master and his Friend:
but Dermaid checked him, in his quiet way,
and told him the story of that mounting day,
the omens and the portents, one by one,

from the sun's rising to the setting sun.

DERMAID: And when we both came out of the dusty barn
the Abbot's tired eyes blinked, his step was slow,
and 'Master' says I, 'You have made us sad
so often speaking of your early going
into the shadowy place.' And he replied
'I too am sad although I have no right,
knowing the waiting joy, for now and then
I have an unredeemed delight in living.'

MOCHONNA: It's a great pity he would not stay quiet
but must come hirpling out to the busy fields.

DERMAID: You know the temper of Columcille. I begged
him to stay
but he kept on ... the rising threat of rain,
the harvest must be saved ... his part was prayer.
He could not leave his little family
to bear the weight alone.

MOCHONNA: Still, if I'd been here, or Bahan even,
he might have stayed at peace: the rocky road
has jolted his old heart. He looks far-through.

DERMAID: But he will not die yet.

MOCHONNA: Why not?

DERMAID: I have his word,
and he was always exact in prophecy.

MOCHONNA: What was his word?

DERMAID: I have no right to tell;
but he is safe asleep for this black hour.

MOCHONNA: Should I not call the brothers?

DERMAID: There's no need yet. Stay quietly with me.
The rush and clamour would disturb his rest.
He'd wake and bid them to the fields again.
Being vexed at the burden of his clogging heart
he'd try to rise. Sit quietly and watch.

MOCHONNA: Now lying here, he is not like the man
who thundered judgment to the Northern Kings.
A stormy saint. How came he by his name?
I've always wondered why it was Columcille ...
for Columcille must mean the Dove of the Church.
He was no Dove: he did not coo nor croon

      but lived with vigour: even in his prayer
      he never mumbled with an old man's drone,
      but spoke straight out to God. He was no Dove.
DERMAID: Yet he was gentle, never meshed in guile
      —but peace! our voices rasp against his rest.
      [*Music: singing of monks—fading-out, childish voices babbling and
      lilting, fading-out.*]
MOCHONNA: Is it yet time? I have not heard the bell.
DERMAID: Nor will a while. In truth you fell asleep
      over my story of how I brought him back
      from his last blessing of the well-stacked barn,
      of how he still had strength to climb the hill
      and look upon Iona and bless its limits.
COLUMCILLE: For thirty years now you have harboured me;
      my thanks, good little island, blessed Iona,
      and from this peak Lord Christ has let me see
      the pagan darkness coil and scatter back
      before the little light that we have held,
      our torch for truth, that when the true dawn comes
      must shrink and gutter in the shining air.
      An old man's blessing on you; may your stones
      remain to show a wide enfranchised world
      that tho' we failed for weakness, in our hearts
      we willed much good, and wrought some, and believed
      the purposes of breath were not in vain.
DERMAID: So having spoken, Columcille turned back
      leaning on me, we at length achieved
      the wall, the gate, this threshold, and, at last,
      this cold stone cupboard. But he would not rest.
      I tried to urge him. But he still had time
      to write a little. He had promised himself,
      and no day, not even the last, was ever complete
      without its task of writing.
COLUMCILLE [*on echo*]: It shall serve for others. I myself have
      gathered much delight and sense from books. I owe to these
      who wrote for me that I should keep their words
      still legible for other eyes than mine.
      Give me my pen, good Dermaid. I shall write;
      and lay the Psalter on the sloping board,

beside the page half-written.
'They that seek the Lord shall not fail in every good.'
Here I must pause. It is the end of the page;
let Bahan write what follows. I am weary.

DERMAID: And so I sanded the parchment and laid it there,
and helped him to his bench and wrapped him as close
as his old cowhide quilt allowed,
and waited by him till you came.

MOCHONNA: He asked for no one, knowing he will die?
I shall be blamed for this when it is over.
There are those that have the right to be beside him.

DERMAID: Who more than any? And yet he will not die
here, in his place, but in full service in the church.

MOCHONNA: He told you more than you admit to me.
He loved you, Dermaid, so I believe you to the end.
I shall go to matins, and there tell the others.
Fetch us at once, if he should seem to wake.

DERMAID: You do not believe me. *He* shall come to *you.*
[*The bell sounds: noises of distant shuffling and quiet gabble and
then quiet singing behind.*]

COLUMCILLE: The bell has sounded, Dermaid.

DERMAID: It has, my Master.

COLUMCILLE: Give me your hand, good Dermaid, I must go.

DERMAID: There, Master. Rest your hand against the wall
and do not try to rise too suddenly,
for you were unsteady before you took your rest.

COLUMCILLE: I'm alright, Dermaid, now. I am ready to go.

DERMAID: Easy, good Master. Lean your weight on me.
Now easy, easy—I never thought I'd be
a staff for Columcille.

COLUMCILLE: Not since I was small
did I require this service.

DERMAID: Rest here awhile, my Master, by the door,
to summon strength.

COLUMCILLE: I leave this little cell,
that has contained so many of my rich days,
now for the last time.

DERMAID: You leave so much;
fasting and prayer and writing and meditation,

but you carry with you the love that the world has poured
into its narrow well.

COLUMCILLE: And I carry the dreams—
the restless coil of dreams has jostled my sleep.
You have heard me wake and cry out because of those
dreams.
Now I am rested. I must go alone.
No, Dermaid. I alone. You must remain.

DERMAID: But Master—

COLUMCILLE: You shall come in your own time
where I go now. And I shall welcome you—
[*Singing louder*]

DERMAID: The habit stays. I always must obey.
Yet spare a stirrup-blessing for your son—
He does not heed me, hear me. He's so intent
on the hard journey. Slowly now he drags—
He's past the threshold, moving towards the lights.
Now he sways; and I not there. He totters.
But Bahan sees him.
[*Singing stops abruptly*]
He comes towards the Saint.
O mercy, Christ. He falls, the old man falls
on his stiff knees, and sprawls across the flagstones.
He moves his hands in blessing. The others,
Mochonna and the rest, they run to him.
Bahan's arms are about him.
The stiff arm drops.
He lays the old head down. O ours no more,
my master belongs to the timeless, the ageless Glory.
[*While* AXALL *is speaking, solemn music behind rises slowly in
triumphant crescendo.*]

AXALL: I who leaned about him cannot follow,
so sheer the strong Dove's flight into the light,
strong as the eagle, swift as curving swallow,
bright as the first star in approaching night;
forgotten now the rages, spent and over
the turbulence of poets and of kings;
the white soul leaps to greet her Lord and Lover,
and Mercy falls upon the mounting wings.

JOHN HEWITT

EX·LIBRIS